The Open Brethren: A Christian Sect
in the Modern World

Peter Herriot

The Open Brethren: A Christian Sect in the Modern World

palgrave
macmillan

Peter Herriot
Birkbeck, University of London
London, UK

ISBN 978-3-030-03218-0   ISBN 978-3-030-03219-7   (eBook)
https://doi.org/10.1007/978-3-030-03219-7

Library of Congress Control Number: 2018960939

Cover design: Tjaša Krivec

This Palgrave Macmillan imprint is published by the registered company Springer Nature Switzerland AG
The registered company address is: Gewerbestrasse 11, 6330 Cham, Switzerland

ACKNOWLEDGEMENTS

I thank my cousins David and Nigel Fulton and Walter Herriot, and also the publisher's reviewers, for their helpful suggestions. Particular thanks to my wife, Barbara.

ABOUT THE BOOK

What happens when an academic psychologist starts examining the Bible which his father left to him in his will? The handwritten notes in its margins reveal in extraordinary detail the belief system of the Open Plymouth Brethren, a sect in which the author was brought up. They rekindle long-forgotten memories and force him to try to make sense of the Brethren from his personal experience as well as from his preferred academic perspective.

This, then, is a book written from multiple perspectives, grounded in social science theory and concepts, but illustrated by vivid accounts of the Brethren from their own mouths and the occasional personal anecdote.

Peter Herriot argues that the Brethren are important because, at least in their more conservative faction, they constitute a perfect example of a fundamentalism. Their culture is entirely opposed to the beliefs, values, and norms of modernity. As a result, they challenge modern Christianity, and impede its efforts to engage with global society.

CONTENTS

About the Author

Peter Herriot was brought up in a Plymouth Brethren family, and is now a liberal Methodist. He enjoyed an academic career, specializing in organizational and social psychology. Since retirement, he has written on religious fundamentalism from a social psychological perspective. Among his books are *Religious Fundamentalism and Social Identity* (2008); *Religious Fundamentalism: Global, Local, and Personal* (2009); and *Warfare and Waves: Calvinists and Charismatics in the Church of England* (2017).

CHAPTER 1

Introduction

Oldershaw Old Boys Football Club played in Wallasey, Cheshire, UK. You could tell that Wallasey was one of the posher suburbs of Liverpool because the club did not feel the need to insert the word 'Rugby' before 'Football'. Rugby is, after all, the only game which young Wallasey gentlemen would play.

The club was enjoying considerable success in the season 1930–1, and by 21 March, its record was: Played 24, Won 13, Drawn 7, Lost 4. Contributing to this sterling performance was my father, Frank Henry Herriot, then aged 22, who played in the scrum half position. However, on his copy of the fixture card, the results for the remaining three fixtures of the season remain blank.

The explanation for this omission possibly lies in an event which immediately and completely changed the course of his life. As he strolled along the promenade at New Brighton after the match, he spotted a knot of people down on the beach. Curious as to what they were doing, he went down to find out. They turned out to be members of a fundamentalist Christian sect known popularly as the Plymouth Brethren,[1] and they were very persuasively seeking to make converts, so persuasively, indeed, that my father, a polite and obliging young man, got converted.

From then on, his life was dominated by his adherence to the Brethren. Soon after my father joined the local Brethren 'assembly' [church congregation], the Great Depression ravaged the nation's economy, and he had to move to London to find a job as an accountant. The Liverpool Brethren

© The Author(s) 2018
P. Herriot, *The Open Brethren: A Christian Sect in the Modern World*,
https://doi.org/10.1007/978-3-030-03219-7_1

found him lodgings with a hospitable Brethren family with eight children, four boys and four girls, in Hackney in the East End of London. The inevitable happened and Frank and Ada fell in love. Of the eight siblings, my mother was one of the six who continued to share their parents' religious allegiance; the two oldest brothers rebelled. And so another Brethren family began. The first verse of the hymn which concluded their wedding service ran as follows:

> This marriage union now complete,
> The twain are one in wedlock sweet;
> Oh, guide them, Father, with Thine eye,
> Until they reach their home on high.

Soon after my birth, as their first and only child, the Second World War disturbed the fledgling family's equilibrium. On being conscripted, my father was faced with a dilemma. He was a conservative, conscientious, and patriotic person who took seriously his obligations as a citizen. Yet at the same time, he was convinced that his allegiance to the Brethren required him to obey the biblical commandment not to kill. His solution was to register as a conscientious objector, but only in so far as active combat was concerned. In its wisdom, the Royal Air Force commissioned him as an accountant officer whose task was to pay the airmen their wages. God and nation were reconciled, but at the cost of paying others to do what he was unwilling to do himself. However, this apparent moral difficulty did not seem to trouble him, perhaps because he could construe conscription as a requirement of the powers that be, whom Scripture enjoined him to obey. Anyway, he accepted and retained his service medals. I have them still.

Such dilemmas were not to recur with any regularity during the rest of my father's life. This was because his time was spent almost entirely in three social situations: his work, his immediate and extended family, and his local Brethren assembly. The latter two were related, in the sense that his family in London consisted of his in-laws, who were nearly all Brethren (and Sisters). His own family remained in Liverpool.

At work, he was the ideal employee for a traditional and hierarchical firm of merchant traders in the City of London: reliable, honest, loyal, and a team player. He remained with the same employer until he retired. The same virtues characterized his life in the Brethren, to the extent that before long he was invited to become one of 'the oversight', that is, a small group of male Brethren who direct affairs within each local assembly.

This prominent position resulted in a major sacrifice of his time and effort. First, there was the expected attendance at Monday evening's Prayer Meeting, Wednesday's 'Ministry' Meeting [teaching from the Bible], the occasional conference with other assemblies on Saturdays, the 'Breaking of Bread' [worship and Holy Communion] on Sunday morning, and the 'Gospel Meeting' [preaching for conversions] on Sunday evening. Then there were the meetings of the oversight, together with the leadership responsibilities attached. And finally, there were evangelistic efforts to which my father felt obliged to contribute, remembering perhaps the nature of his own conversion. These included such events as the provision of 'the gospel message' and a meal (in that order) at hostels for impoverished men in the East End of London, or the conduct of open-air services in public places.

As a consequence of his demanding role, my father had little time for any sort of social or cultural life. Many cultural forms, such as cinema, theatre, concerts, and dancing, were disapproved of by the Brethren anyway, but he found time to watch the occasional sporting event, while my mother found solace in the Romantic poets. All social activities and nearly all friendships were Brethren-based. Where they were not, the conversion of the 'unsaved' friends was always lurking somewhere on the agenda.

Retirement to the South Coast of England did offer a degree of opportunity for leisure, bowls for my father and painting for my mother. But the local assembly continued to make demands, especially of the former. Brethren worship is conducted not by a minister or priest, but by the men in the congregation, who preach or pray or choose a hymn 'as the Spirit leads'. There were soon only two or three elderly brethren in the ageing and dwindling congregation. My father touchingly notes in the margin of his Bible next to the book of the prophet Zephaniah, chapter 3, verse 17: "Len Wicks ministered on this verse after the Lord's Supper [Holy Communion] on 30.6.1991. He was called home [died] the next day". Father's contribution was thus essential for the assembly to continue to function.

While the other brethren spoke spontaneously and without feeling the need for specific preparation, my father lacked the confidence to do so. He also liked structure and predictability, so instead of sharing his impromptu reflections with the congregation, he used notes when speaking which he had previously written in his Bible. Together with the rugby club fixture list and an autographed scorecard of the 1948 Australian cricket tourists, this Bible was one of the very few documents which I inherited from him. His handwritten notes in its margins provide the impetus for the rest of this book.

So, how can one possibly make sense of the story I have just told? My immediate response was to revert to my own formation and experience, and apply a systematic social psychological analysis, resulting in an academic text. But I soon realized that I had already crossed a line in the academic sand. I had already used the first-person singular in telling the above story more frequently than in my entire career in academia! There was now no possibility of following the rules. I would simply have to find a more inclusive and comprehensive way of understanding my father's life and my own upbringing.

I realized that I had been attracted to the story because my attention had been caught by the mementos which I had inherited. One of the first principles of any attempt to understand people is to pay careful attention to what they say and write about themselves. If I was to do justice to an account of the Brethren, I would have to read and listen from their own perspective. However, I did not have to implant myself in a Brethren assembly to do so, like some intrepid twenty-first-century Margaret Mead with her Samoan Islanders. Participant observation, in my case involuntary, had already occurred, and a Brethren upbringing never leaves one.

So, the first perspective to be taken was that of the Brethren themselves. What was their view of the world and of their own place in it? How did they think about the past, the present, and the future? How did they seek to understand the transcendent, and what role did they think God played in history and in daily life? I was soon to appreciate more fully the extraordinary influence of the Bible on the Brethren perspective.

But to limit myself to the Brethren's own account would be to imitate them in their utter reliance on the Bible: I would be basing my understanding on a single perspective only. I had only to reflect for a moment to realize the profound effect which my subsequent academic formation as a psychologist has had on my own narrative. A social scientific perspective would impact on my attempts to understand my own upbringing and my father's life whether I wanted it to or not. And I certainly wanted to understand.

I also recognized that a third perspective would affect my narrative as well: my own subsequent religious development and current adherence. As a liberal Methodist, I am, to put it mildly, at a considerable theological distance from the Brethren. However, the journey from there to here and the distance travelled provide another vantage point from which to view them.

As a result of these reflections, I ventured on my exploration of my father's Bible, recognizing that my own experience, social science, and theology were inevitably going to affect my conclusions about what I found there. This recognition resulted in a novel structure for this book, which I will outline below.

So what did his Bible look like, and what clues would it give regarding my father's, and the Brethren's, beliefs? It certainly is a handsome thing. It sports a soft leather cover, with a gold title on the spine, overlapping edges, and turned-over corners, made by William Yapp, Brethren publishers (founded 1853). It is, of course, the Authorised (or 'King James') Version, strongly favoured by the Brethren over other more recent translations. All 1500 pages are printed on wafer-thin India paper, and have wide margins to facilitate notes. In addition, there are 24 lined blank pages bound into the text at front and back.

This design was entirely suited to the way a brother's Bible would be used. It had to be frequently transported from home to assembly and back, so it had to be as small and light as possible. Moreover, when 'taking part', a brother had to stand up from his seat, holding his Bible open in one hand so as to be able to refer to the passage being considered, and in my father's case, to his marginal notes. The overlapping edges of the cover protected the pages, although many Brethren used a Bible bag to transport their copy. Others carried it uncovered, believing that this was a 'witness to the unsaved'.

My first big surprise came when I started to read the marginal notes. These were to be found on most pages of both Old and New Testaments, however unpromising the text appeared for use in public worship. I soon realized that they did not consist, as one might expect, of explanations of the text, discussion of the issues which it raised, or applications to the Christian's daily life. Rather, they were paraphrases or summaries of the passage, adding little additional meaning or commentary. Where they did refer to any other material, this was in the form of references to other related passages in the Bible.

A further surprise was the prevalence of alliteration in my father's notes. For example, he summarizes chapters 4–10 of St Luke's Gospel as follows:
Service in the Light of the Cross:

(i) Its Commencement – the Claim of Jesus to be Christ (ch4 vv14-44)
(ii) Its Course – the Claim contested and condemned (5/1–6/11)
(iii) Its Consummation – the Claim considered and certified (6/12–8/56)
(iv) Its Conclusion – the Claim confessed and confirmed (9/vv1-50)

I later realized that this fondness for alliteration is a feature of Brethren commentary, and permeates the several devotional magazines which circulate among them.

Why was my father (and why were other Brethren) so unwilling to go beyond the text? Why did they exercise such ingenuity in devising alliterative headings which added nothing to meaning, and only a little to memorability? Psychologists Ralph Hood, Peter Hill, and Paul Williamson offer an answer.[2] It lies in the principle of *intratextuality*. That is, Brethren believe that the text itself, the Bible, determines how it ought to be read and understood. It speaks for itself. So when that text tells us that it is the Word of God, we must conclude that the text is sacred, and that it therefore imparts absolute truths. Clearly, when God speaks it must be true. What point is there in adding to God's Word with words of merely human origin? The truth is to be found in the text, and all that the preacher should do is to structure and summarize it to make it more accessible and memorable. The text speaks to us directly, or rather, God speaks to us, provided we are listening. Hood's account explains why the Reformation principle of *sola scriptura* ('by Scripture alone') plays such an immensely important part in Brethren belief and practice.

It was not only the form of my father's notes which caused my initial surprise, however. It was also his choice of the biblical passages which he should annotate. There was for a start a strong emphasis on both the Israelites of the Old Testament and the young church of the New as a faithful few, a persecuted remnant, but with a special covenant relationship with God. They were firmly distinguished from the heathen (OT) and the unsaved (NT), for the latter a boundary which could be crossed only by a conversion experience.

This emphasis on *separation and purity* was matched by the idea of *authority*. The faith was the eternal truth, 'once for all delivered unto the saints' (Jude 1:3), and therefore unchangeable in doctrine or practice. My father's notes place particular emphasis on church order. He assumes that St Paul's directions to the various early churches are God's directions to Christians everywhere and at any time.

The words of the Bible are taken at their "immediate and obvious" literal meaning, with such consequent problems as talking serpents and donkeys, demons and angels, and the saints being taken up bodily in the air to ascend to heaven with Christ at the time of the rapture. The possibility that my father may have had some difficulty in accepting wholeheartedly this view of the Bible is demonstrated by the subjects covered in his extensive notes on the blank pages. It is as if he anticipates having to address these issues in public as well as in private. Subjects of these essays include the prophecies of the end times, Old Testament morality, women in the church, and literal versus figurative interpretations of the Bible.

So, even the very first piece of evidence about the Brethren indicated that it would be impossible to understand them by using their own perspective alone. It would be impossible because I could never succeed in banishing my own perspectives from my investigations. But more important, it would also be impossible because closed belief systems cannot be properly understood on their own terms, for there is nothing left with which to explain them. Other perspectives have to be brought to bear.

Each academic discipline that is relevant can contribute its own work. The outstanding example in the case of the Brethren is Tim Glass's masterly account of their history.[1] But it is only when different perspectives are brought to bear on the same issues that a holistic understanding can be reached. And what are those issues? Why, in other words, is it important *in general,* rather than just to the author, to understand the Brethren? It is because the Brethren (or rather, a faction of them) represent a perfect example of a fundamentalism.

And why do we need such an archetypical example? Most research on fundamentalism, in contrast, has covered a wide variety of religious movements and sects in an effort to discover its definitive features. My argument is that in essence fundamentalism consists of a total rejection of modernity. The violence which characterizes a few fundamentalisms is definitely not the main issue, despite its emphasis by the media. Rather, fundamentalism is important because its world view is incompatible with the modern world. In its implacable opposition to the beliefs, values, and social norms which constitute modernity's prospectus, it directs our attention to our current failure to fulfil that prospectus. For the Brethren, this opposition is expressed, not by violent action or by political activism, but by withdrawal and separation.

The second definitive characteristic of fundamentalism which the Brethren demonstrate perfectly is their attribution of total authority to their holy book, in their case the Bible. The idea that the Bible is God's Word speaking directly to each of them is the central belief from which their entire complex belief system follows. In a logical and consistent way, they draw conclusions about what they should believe and how they should act solely from the text itself.

My aim, then, is to gain a deeper insight into the Brethren as a fundamentalism by using different perspectives from which to view it. What does it feel like to hold a completely counter-cultural world view, and how is such a world view developed and maintained in adherents? How is their belief system structured and justified? What sort of psychological benefits and rewards accrue from belonging? Which societal contexts enable fundamentalisms to exist? To what extent do they succeed in separating themselves from a networked world? And most important of all, how do fundamentalisms hinder mainstream religion from providing its potential benefits for the global social system?

These are big questions with which to burden a relatively small Protestant sect. Yet it is perhaps possible to get some traction on them by means of a detailed and multi-perspective immersion in their life and culture. I have tried to structure the book so as to enable such an experience. The first four chapters are written as if they are the writings of different categories of person, each of which is likely to have a different perspective on the Brethren. Thus the first is written in the style of the 'tight', or conservative, faction of the Open Brethren. Both style and content are derived from the publications of this faction. The second is similar, but speaks for the 'loose', or more liberal, faction. The third gives an outline historical account as if by a professional historian, and the fourth similarly from a social scientist. Chapter 5, in fact, represents how I would have written the entire book if I had stuck to the academic rules.

All the first four chapters have the word 'Tale' in their titles. This is not an arrogant pretence to emulate Geoffrey Chaucer and *The Canterbury Tales*, but a pointer to the fact that all four are written in an attempt to capture the language and assumptions of each different category of person. Chapters 6 and 7, on the other hand, come directly from the words of the Brethren themselves, from their own obituaries and testimonies.

Parts II and III constitute the book's core analysis, of the Brethren emphases on authority and on separation, respectively. They are from the author's own perspective, so have a heavy social scientific content, but with some theological and personal reflections included as well. The consideration of *authority* permits the detailed exploration of the Brethren belief system; that of *separation* leads to discussion of identities and self. The detail in Part II comes from close analysis of the Brethren's intratextual use of the Bible, and from their patriarchal attitude to women. In Part III, it concerns the ways in which they withdraw from the world, from other Christians, and even from other Brethren with whom they disagree.

Part IV looks at the bigger picture. First, I try to establish that the Brethren are indeed a fundamentalism, albeit one which withdraws from the rest of the world rather than seeking to influence it. I then contrast the

Brethren with the modernity to which they are so hostile, noting that mainstream Christianity (and religion generally) is one of the modern world's global social systems. Fundamentalism can indeed hinder religion's integrative mission in the world, but ongoing dialogue between religion and the other global social systems can, I conclude, overcome its disruptive potential.

I should emphasize that the first four chapters present a varied set of perspectives on the Brethren *as a whole*. They include accounts of how the Brethren movement split into the Open and Exclusive sects, and also of how the Open Brethren developed two factions in the twentieth century, the 'tight' and 'loose' factions. The rest of the book, however, deals only with the tight faction. This is because of my desire to use the Brethren as a 'pure' instance of fundamentalism, so as to shed light on fundamentalism as an important type of religious movement.

Fortunately there are many alternatives for those who are disappointed by this limited approach. I have already referenced Tim Glass's monumental history of the Open Brethren.[1] Those who would have liked a biography of my father or others of his generation will enjoy sociologist Richard Sennett's masterpiece *The Corrosion of Character*,[3] which mourns the decay of their currently less fashionable virtues. Others might seek accounts of how a Brethren upbringing can affect people's lives, a recent riveting example of which is Rebecca Stott's *In the Days of Rain*.[4]

What remains is my own narrative, for which I take total responsibility. All mistakes and unintentionally patronizing comments are down to me. Readers will doubtless decide for themselves whether they would have preferred a more traditional academic approach. All I can say is that I have hugely enjoyed writing what follows; but whether my father would have enjoyed reading it is quite another matter. However, he would doubtless have taken it all in his stride.

NOTES

1. Grass, Tim (2006) Gathering to His Name: The Story of Open Brethren in Britain and Ireland. Milton Keynes: Paternoster.
2. Hood, Ralph, Hill, Peter, and Williamson, Paul (2005) The Psychology of Religious Fundamentalism. New York: Guilford Press.
3. Sennett, Richard (1998) The Corrosion of Character: The Personal Consequences of Work in the New Capitalism. New York: Norton.
4. Stott, Rebecca (2017) In the Days of Rain. A Daughter. A Father. A Cult. London: 4th Estate.

PART I

Perspectives

CHAPTER 2

The Tight Brother's Tale

HUMAN HISTORY BC

History is the story of the Almighty God's dealings with mankind. From the very beginning of history, God has sought obedience from, and fellowship with, sinful Man.[1] He offered Adam the Garden of Eden to tend. However, Adam, persuaded by Eve—who had, in her turn, been seduced by Satan—disobeyed God's single prohibition. He ate the forbidden fruit.

Now furnished with a conscience, the knowledge of good and evil, Man failed to heed it. Instead, in the second '*dispensation*', or period of history, the earth was filled with corruption and violence. The Almighty punished these sins by destroying mankind with the Flood, although He preserved Noah and his family as a godly remnant.

Next, in the *third dispensation* of God's dealings with mankind, He bestowed upon him the benefit of government. Man now had not only his individual conscience, but also established laws to guide his conduct. But due to his sinful nature, he still disobeyed and arrogantly sought to reach Heaven by building the Tower of Babel.

Despairing of mankind, God now chose Abraham to be the father of a special people whom He had chosen for His own: Israel. He promised Abraham, in an eternal covenant, both prosperity and a land in Canaan within which to settle. But Israel refused to settle during this *fourth dispensation*, and wandered off into the fleshpots of Egypt.

The ever-faithful Father God rescued His chosen people from their captivity there by the blood of the Passover and by miraculously restraining

© The Author(s) 2018

P. Herriot, *The Open Brethren: A Christian Sect in the Modern World*,
https://doi.org/10.1007/978-3-030-03219-7_2

the Red Sea. On Mount Sinai, He gave them the basis of the *fifth dispensation*, His holy commandments, which they were to keep faithfully. After all, they had been redeemed from Egypt and received special favours as the people of His choice.

Yet, once again, Israel acted according to their fallen nature. Once again, God's chosen people ran after false gods and broke His commandments continuously. Exiled in Assyria and Babylon, they survived only as a remnant, Judah. However, they failed to appreciate the seriousness of their sin, and their inability to keep God's law. They were, consequently, unwilling to humbly accept God's greatest gift, the Messiah, the Lord Jesus Christ.

The entire history of God's dealings with His people, Israel, had pointed towards this amazing culmination of God's grace. However, they blindly failed to recognize the signs and types of Christ which littered their history.[2] Instead, they crucified Him on the Cross of Calvary. Little did they realize that by so doing, they had made possible the salvation of the whole world. Mankind could now be saved through the blood of the Lamb, justification by faith in Christ's sacrifice, rather than by vain attempts to keep God's law (Romans 3.23).

But our Father God raised the Lord Jesus Christ from the tomb, and took Him up into Heaven to rule at His right hand (Hebrews 1.3). Signalling the start of the present *sixth dispensation*, the Church Age, God sent the Holy Spirit on the day of Pentecost to establish His heavenly people, the Church. The Holy Spirit enables us to be free from constant judgement under the earthly law. We are living as God's spiritual, rather than as His earthly people, "destined not for earth, but for heaven".[3] We, not the Jews, are God's Church (Romans 11), and so, our lives are to be given over to His spiritual service. Our spiritual tasks are, first, to exalt the Name of Our Saviour, The Lord Jesus Christ, by remembering Him in the Breaking of Bread and in prayer; and second, to fulfil Christ's Great Commission: "Go ye into all the world, and preach the gospel to every creature" (Matthew 16.15). "Our task is not to try to reform the world, but, by preaching and living the Gospel in godliness, to rescue lost men from suffering eternal punishment in Hell".[4]

The first five dispensations of human history occupied just over 4000 years. We are now fast nearing the end of the sixth, the Church Age. History is reaching its climax, its final and ultimate conclusion, under the divine control of our Eternal God.

THE CHURCH AGE THUS FAR

After Pentecost, the Holy Spirit rapidly empowered believers to gather together unto the Name of the Lord Jesus Christ in local assemblies (Acts 4). They sought to remember Him in the Breaking of Bread and prayers, and also to spread the Gospel of His grace, as He had commanded. The apostles needed to admonish and instruct them in these tasks (e.g. I Corinthians 3&5; Revelation 1–3), but the young assemblies generally flourished and many thousands were saved and added to their number.

Soon, though, Man-made religion began to usurp the work of the Holy Spirit.[5] Its sinful structures and organizations served Mammon rather than God. Allied with the state, the Roman Church grew rich and corrupt. It suppressed all dissent, and kept the people in a state of gross superstition and ignorance of the Holy Scripture. Otherwise they would have realized that salvation was by faith alone in the precious Blood of the Lamb, not by the performance of priestly rituals and daily penances.

But throughout the Church Age, the precious silver thread of the true faith as taught by the apostles has continued to run through history.[6] A holy remnant of true believers kept the faith alive. Their history has been suppressed by the Roman Church, but down the ages, such courageous disciples as the Waldensians and the Moravians kept the flame of revealed truth burning. The Reformation of the sixteenth century with its great message of justification by faith alone, and its emphasis on Holy Scripture as God's Word, turned the little flame into a great fire. Next, the Methodist revival in the eighteenth century led to an increased emphasis on the importance of holiness for the believer and in the Church.

Alas, these wonderful outpourings of God's Holy Spirit were hampered by a failure, inspired by Satan, the Prince of Darkness, to return to the purity and simplicity of the apostolic church. Despite the clear evidence of spiritual gifts in all believers, control was still exercised by clerical hierarchies and religious structures. The pure model of the New Testament assembly remained obscured by the power of the sects. For that is what the so-called 'Christian' denominations really are—sects which have broken away from the one true apostolic church and imposed Man's systems onto the pure work of the Holy Spirit.

But, thanks be to God, there arose in the early nineteenth century a movement inspired by the Holy Spirit.[7] He revealed to several groups of godly Christians in Ireland and England the enduring truths of the New Testament regarding the real nature of the church and how it should be ordered (Acts 2.42). Grasping the biblical truth of the priesthood of all believers, these saints gathered together in local assemblies, forsaking any existing allegiance they may have had to a specific sect.

In line with this separation, they went back to the Scriptures afresh to discern God's rules for assemblies. With the Spirit's guidance, they developed a body of Assembly Truth which clearly marked them out from the sects. As well as insisting on New Testament assembly governance and practice, Assembly Truth emphasized the centrality of the Lord's Supper; the adoration of the person of the Lord Jesus Christ; the preaching of His Gospel; and His coming again to rule in glory.

However, over the subsequent two centuries, even the assemblies have failed to maintain their original separation from this present sinful and rebellious world, and from the sects. Ignoring the clear instructions of God's Word, some have involved themselves in the things of this world: materialism, so-called culture and education, and Man's earthly politics and organizations. Their faithfulness in preaching the Gospel and in serving their local assembly has diminished.[8] Instead, they have heretically allied themselves with all manner of sectarian enterprises in the name of the Gospel. Many assemblies have dwindled in numbers, or even closed, as a result. Such disobedience, in association with Man's increasing rebellion against God Himself,[9] is a sure sign that the end times are fast approaching.

THE END TIMES

The *seventh and final dispensation* of human history is the Lord Jesus Christ's direct rule over the world for 1000 years.[10] He will exercise this *millennial* rule from Jerusalem, and it will be a time of perfect peace and governance. Order will at last be restored to the world. Israel will inherit the whole of the Promised Land and become the leading nation on earth. The seventh dispensation is mankind's last chance to obey God and worship Him alone. It obviously constitutes an unarguable reason for eagerly seizing this chance.

However, after the 1000 years are over, Satan will emerge from the abyss into which he had been cast to lead a final rebellion against God and His saints. He will seduce many to join his army, and God, having defeated him, will finally conclude that Man is incurably sinful. He will judge the rebels seated on His Great White Throne, bringing this sinful world to its final end and creating a new heaven and a new earth where righteousness will dwell unchallenged.[11]

But before the millennium begins,[12] the Lord Jesus Christ will return to earth, down through the heavens and then in the air. He will come to transport all believers, resurrected or living, back up to rule with Him in the heavenly places, where they will gaze upon His face in adoration and gratitude. Then, after this *Rapture*, but still before the millennium starts, God will visit upon seven years of appalling suffering on earth, the dreaded *Tribulation*, before he defeats Satan at Armageddon and banishes him to the abyss.

The Church Age, the sixth dispensation, thus ends with two dramatic events—the Rapture and the Tribulation. Our sure knowledge from Scripture that they will occur creates both eager anticipation and an incredible sense of urgency. We can be joyful that we will soon be transported from this wicked and sinful world to see our Saviour face-to-face.

> Christian, though the world about us,
> May give us good cause to fear,
> Let the words of scripture cheer us,
> Christ's return is very near.
>
> Cast your eyes not down, dejected,
> At the state of things down here,
> Lift your heads, and look to heaven,
> Whence our Lord shall soon appear.[13]

But we cannot linger in such anticipatory longing and delight. Rather, we must all the more fervently preach the Gospel with our lips and in our lives, for who knows when the Lord will return?[14] The unsaved will then be condemned to unimaginable torment, a fate of which they are totally unaware unless they hear the Word of salvation. What a responsibility is ours!

ASSEMBLY TRUTH

Our only hope of meeting such responsibility is to steadfastly maintain "the faith once for all delivered to the saints" (Jude 1.3). We must uphold Assembly Truth, for it is through the local assembly that sinners are converted and disciples developed. God has given us crystal clear instructions in Scripture on how to establish and maintain New Testament assemblies. Indeed, the justification for assembly practices is that each one is explicitly sanctioned by the Word of God. We ignore the New Testament pattern at our peril.

This pattern is simple, powerful, and different.[15] It is directed by the Holy Spirit rather than by Man's authority. Assemblies are to have no denominational title; we are simply local believers gathered unto the Name of the Lord.[16] We have no organizational structure beyond the local assembly. We employ no priests or ministers, for every believer has a spiritual ministry. No unbelievers are part of our fellowship, and only those in fellowship in the assembly can share in the Breaking of Bread: for we are admonished, "Come out from among them and be ye separate" (2 Corinthians 6.17).

We must make certain that no false or heretical teaching is allowed to creep in and corrupt the assembly's testimony. All visitors are therefore expected to provide a letter of commendation from another assembly, vouching for the soundness of their doctrine and the godliness of their witness.[17] False teaching and error are unlikely to pollute all the assemblies, since each assembly is independent. If there were a central authority for the Satan to infiltrate, false doctrine would be broadcast to every congregation and spread like wildfire.

Rather, each assembly has its own governance, consisting of elders who form the *oversight*.[18] Such leadership is a grace, a gift from God. It is not a natural talent, or the result of education or training. Still less is it the outcome of a democratic vote by the assembly fellowship. No, elders are appointed by the Holy Spirit Himself. When He calls upon a Brother to serve as an elder, He equips him to do so.

It is the sacred responsibility of the elders to ensure that the saints continue steadfastly in the purity and simplicity of New Testament worship and practice (Acts 2.42). Any venture over and above what the Scripture expressly permits is a slippery slope indeed.[19] Brethren are to take vocal part in worship as they are led by the Spirit and enjoined by Scripture, but there is no justification for the use of music or drama or any other such modern entertainments. The purpose of worship is to please God, not Man.

The elders must ensure that nothing is done that is not enjoined by Scripture. But they must, above all, prevent anything which the Bible expressly forbids. It states absolutely unequivocally that Sisters are to keep silent in assembly meetings and cover their heads (1 Corinthians 11.1–15). They are subject to their husbands in the same way as the church is subject to the Lord Jesus Christ.[20] The modern scourge of feminism has grown so powerful in our culture that some assemblies are even heretically allowing Sisters to participate audibly in worship and to wear immodest clothing in the house of God.[21]

But it is not only in the assemblies that our arch foe, the Satan, has gained a foothold—he is indeed 'the enemy within'. He has also infiltrated the sects, together with various evangelical movements which claim to spread the 'Christian' gospel.[22] All the sects propagate some poisonous false doctrine or other—infant baptism, or non-scriptural sacraments, or so-called charismatic worship.[23] Or they deny the inerrancy of Scripture, or the reality of Hell Fire.[24] And as for the movements, they force assembly believers to compromise Bible truth in order to present a united front with members of the sects. The sound brother will refuse to be "unequally yoked together with unbelievers" (2 Corinthians, 6.14) in any such unscriptural enterprise.

No, it is from the assembly that the clarion call of the Gospel to repent and be saved should ring forth. Brethren should devote their entire energies to assembly service.[25] Then and only then will the great days of revival return,[26] and many will be added unto the Lord.

This Is the Word of the Lord

But how can we possibly know all this about the world's future? And why are we so confident that we understand God's will for His church? The answer, of course, lies in Scripture, the inerrant source of all truth.[27] As Brother W.E. Vine has so powerfully put it:

> The faith is contained in the Bible as we have it handed down to us. To attempt to add to it or readjust it or to issue additional decrees as if they were of divine authority, is to impugn the perfect work of the Holy Spirit and to be guilty of presumptuous impiety.......the teachings of the apostles are the standard by which to judge what is true or false in doctrine. Therefore what is not corroborated by the New Testament has not the authority of God.[28]

Scripture is the unchanging and eternal Word of God to us as believers. It was, of course, originally written in languages now no longer in use. God's plan determined that Scripture cannot now be interpreted with new and mistaken meanings as our living language changes.[29] We have the Authorised Version, which gives an accurate sense of the original documents, a sense which does not change over time.

The Holy Spirit inspired the writers of the books of the Bible down to the level of each word.[30] Of course, each writer had his own style, but the Holy Spirit inspired him as an individual to use that style to express the Word of God, and only the Word of God. We should always approach the text assuming it means what it says and says what it means. Since God is speaking to us, He is not going to make it as hard as possible to grasp His meaning. If Scripture does not mean what it says, how can we hope to know what it is about? The moment we abandon the literal sense, we are adrift and uncertain.[31]

Of course, we must not take every passage completely literally. The writers used different genres such as narrative, poetry, and doctrine. They employed figures of speech such as simile, metaphor, and personification.[32] Rather, we should simply approach the text in a common-sense and natural way, recognizing figures of speech for what they are, but seeing the obvious meaning rather than searching for some airy-fairy abstract concept. This applies to narrative passages, where mere human wisdom would balk at the idea of serpents and asses speaking, angels eating, devils entering the bodies of pigs, and the Lord Jesus Christ bodily ascending into Heaven, and much later, returning bodily to earth.[33] But Scriptural truth was not created by the will and imagination of Man; rather, it was revealed to Man by the Holy Spirit of God. Scientists scoff at the Scriptural account of Creation, but how can a mere theory such as evolution match the powerful factual detail of Genesis?[34,35]

Rather, "all Scripture is given by inspiration of God, and is profitable for doctrine, for reproof, for correction, for instruction in righteousness" (2 Timothy 3.16). All its precepts are to be honoured and obeyed by believers, in every department of their lives—family, business, church, and world.[36] We are to take prophecy in its direct literal sense, and act in the light of the signs of the times, indicating as they do the imminence of the Rapture and of the Tribulation to follow. We are to consider the injunctions of Paul and other apostles to the New Testament churches as direct instructions to ourselves in this modern and decadent age. We are to believe the Bible "comes to us with as real an intention as if it came with the direction of our name upon it, fresh from heaven".[37]

We may not always be able to justify our practices by quoting a specific chapter and verse of Scripture. But if we cannot, we should always be able to supply an argument from general Scriptural principles and teaching.[38] There is no room for things to be done because they are enshrined in traditional assembly doctrine or practice if they have no Scriptural justification. Rather, let us always return to the inspirational power and eternal truth of the final arbiter: the Word of God.

Summary

Human history is the story of how sinful Man has consistently disobeyed his Father God. We are now approaching the end of its penultimate era, the Church Age. Even after God sent His Son for man's salvation and His Holy

Spirit for his inspiration, he has strayed from God's Word. Only a remnant has continued to worship in the pure New Testament pattern. But our Lord will soon return, to rapture these true believers back with him into heaven. We must remain faithful to His Word, the Bible, by converting those who have been seduced by rampant sin or false doctrine, and by keeping ourselves pure and separate to be our Saviour's Bride.

NOTES

1. Davis, Malcolm (2016) God's Programme of Seven Ages for Mankind. *Believer's Magazine*, October.
2. Newell, David (2008) A Series of Letters on Bible Study (4): Recognising the Genres. *Believer's Magazine*, November.
3. Davis, Malcolm (2006) The Christian's Hope (3). *Believer's Magazine*, November.
4. See 1 (above).
5. Cargill, R. (2012) Torchbearers of the Truth: Carrying the Torch Today. *Believer's Magazine*, August.
6. Broadbent, E.H. (1931, republished 1985) The Pilgrim Church. Basingstoke: Pickering and Inglis.
7. MacKay, Harold (1986) That the World May Know. Bath: Echoes of Service. Retrieved from www.believershome.com/who-are-the-brethren
8. Editorial (2005) *Precious Seed*, vol. 60, no. 2.
9. Parmenter, Eric (1999) Today's World; Its Character and Climax. *Precious Seed*, vol. 54, no. 4.
10. Hay, J. (2011) An Introduction to Bible Prophecy (7): The Millennium. *Believer's Magazine*, December.
11. Davis, Malcolm (2016) The Development of my Convictions concerning Prophecy: A Personal Testimony. *Believer's Magazine*, June.
12. Davis, Malcolm (2014) The Practical Effects of Prophetic Interpretation. *Precious Seed*, vol. 69, no. 3.
13. Hartley, H. (1994) Quotes: Blessed Hope. *Assembly Testimony*, November/December.
14. Editorial (2005) *Precious Seed*, vol. 60, no. 2.
15. Hay, Jack (2011) Which Church Should I Join, and Why? *Precious Seed*, vol. 66, no. 3.
16. Vine, W.E. (1986) That the World May Know. Bath: Echoes of Service. Retrieved from: www.believershome.com/who-are-the-brethren
17. Cooper, Ken (2012) Letters of Commendation (2). *Believer's Magazine*, May.
18. Editorial (2011) The Elder and the Role of Leadership in the Local Church. *Precious Seed*, vol. 66, no. 2.

19. Sweetnam, M. (2014) The Church of God: The Passion it Declares. *Believer's Magazine,* May.
20. Summers, A. (2013) New Testament Symbols: Paper 6, The Head Covering, Part 2. *Assembly Testimony,* September–October.
21. Sinclair, A. (2007) The Message from the Seven Churches for Today (5). *Believer's Magazine,* June.
22. Cargill, R. (2012) Torchbearers of the Truth: Carrying the Torch Today (2). *Believer's Magazine,* August.
23. Mowat, D. (1996) Tongues and the Bible. *Assembly Testimony,* July–August.
24. Graham, H.W. (1999) Stay In or Come Out: Which? *Assembly Testimony,* November–December.
25. Editorial (2005) *Precious Seed,* vol. 60, no. 2.
26. Editorial (2007) *Precious Seed,* vol. 62, no. 2.
27. Browne, M. (2008) Fundamentalism and the message of the Gospel (1). *Believer's Magazine,* June.
28. Vine, W.E. (1961) The Sufficiency and Finality of Scripture. *Precious Seed,* vol. 12, no. 5.
29. Rogers, E.W. (1989) The Inspiration of Scripture – Part 2. *Assembly Testimony,* March–April.
30. Harding, P. (2015) The Inspiration of Scripture. *Believer's Magazine,* August.
31. Newell, D. (2015) Apocalypse Now. *Believer's Magazine,* January.
32. Newell, D. (2008) A Series of Letters on Bible Study (4): Recognising the Genres. *Believer's Magazine,* November.
33. Browne, M. (2008) Fundamentalism and the message of the Gospel (3): Man – His Sinfulness and Need for Repentance and Faith. *Believer's Magazine,* August.
34. Campbell, Ian (2005) Creation Evangelism. *Precious Seed,* vol. 60, no. 5.
35. Cargill, R.W. (2007) Creation's Story (1): The Creator's Glory. *Believer's Magazine,* January.
36. Ritchie, John (1986) The Bible: Its Divine Inspiration, Absolute Purity, and Supreme Authority. *Assembly Testimony,* May–June.
37. McIntyre, D.M. (2012) Bible Knowledge. *Believer's Magazine,* September.
38. Cooper, K. (2014) The Importance of the Word of God. *Believer's Magazine,* November.

CHAPTER 3

The Loose Brother's Tale

Who We Are

We, Open Brethren, being *Protestant* Christians, are directly descended from that great revolutionary movement, the Reformation.[1] We are founded upon the three great Reformation principles—*sola fide, sola gratia,* and *sola scriptura.* That is, we believe we are saved through faith alone in the redeeming work of Christ (and not by anything we—or anyone else—have done); we are saved only through God's all-sufficient grace and mercy (and not by our failed attempts to keep His laws); and we find the truth as to what to believe and how to act only in God's Word, the Bible (and not in any additional teachings of the institutional church).[2]

But we are not only Protestant Christians: we are *Evangelical* Protestant Christians. That is, we are part of the transformational spiritual movement called Evangelicalism, which gained momentum in the eighteenth century, and ever since has exercised a profound influence on Christianity throughout the world. As their name suggests, Evangelicals' highest priority is to obey Christ's great commission to go out into all the world and make disciples by preaching the gospel of salvation. So great is the urgency of this task that we Evangelicals have put aside the secondary disagreements we have between ourselves in the interests of working together in the great mission with which we have been entrusted. We concentrate, instead, on the shared truths of the gospel, which are the bedrock of the faith and non-negotiable.[3,4]

© The Author(s) 2018

P. Herriot, *The Open Brethren: A Christian Sect in the Modern World,*
https://doi.org/10.1007/978-3-030-03219-7_3

However, we are not only Protestant Evangelical Christians, we are *Open Brethren*. Once again, we are part of a movement of God's Holy Spirit, which—in this case—started in the 1820s. This movement added certain distinctive emphases to Evangelical Protestantism, which we treasure. We strongly believe them to have immediate relevance to today's world.[5] They are encapsulated in the phrase 'unity in diversity'. We believe that God's Church consists of all who truly believe in Christ, and therefore, whatever their differences, all are welcome to our fellowship. We do not exclude people because they do or do not belong to a particular denomination: the sole criterion is their Christian faith. Furthermore, we treat their differences as an asset, for each believer brings their own particular gifts, which God has given to him or her to use in His service.

Open Brethren, then, are Evangelical Protestant Christians. It is no accident that all three elements of this self-description are rightly labelled 'movements'. Change is at the centre of movements—radical change in the status quo, and continuing adaptation to the world in which we find ourselves. We therefore ask ourselves repeated questions about our ideas and practices, while continuing to hold onto the primary truths of the faith.

For example, we are continuously exploring the nature of our *mission* in the world.[6] Are we only to consider the gospel as a matter of introducing individuals to a personal faith in Christ, or do we believe we should concern ourselves at the level of institutions and societies? Are we only concerned with salvation in the hereafter, or do we put a greater stress on the current needs of the world? Do we invite people inside to join us in our sacred activities, or do we participate in their secular ones?

However these discussions pan out, we have to make sure we do not carelessly lose the essence of our faith.[7] Conversion from sin to salvation, and development into discipleship, are our core aims. Our infallible guide is the Holy Spirit speaking through the Bible. It is still essential to maintain the transcendence of the spiritual world over and above the material one. And we must continue to draw the distinction between the sacred and the secular. Only if we are faithful to our heritage will we see the revival we long for. But unless we become better at making meaningful relationships with non-Christians, we will fail.[8]

Aspiration Versus Experience

The original Brethren prospectus is inspiring indeed. To recapitulate, it proclaimed that the Church is the body of believers, not an institution or a building; that the gospel is one of repentance, conversion, and new birth; and that every believer has gifts bestowed upon them by the Holy Spirit to be developed for worship and mission.

However, we have fallen sadly short of these high ideals. We have failed to adapt to our vastly changed social context, instead pretending that practices appropriate in another age will meet the needs of the present secularized generation.[9] The original prospectus can still inspire. Indeed, in its anti-institutional and individualist emphases, it chimes well with the popular *zeitgeist*. But present Brethren practices actively work against the realization of the prospectus.[10]

So, how does the reality contradict the rhetoric? And why does a movement that has contributed so much to the Evangelical faith appear to have lost momentum? One reason lies in its conception of itself as consisting of a group of physically local congregations, each entirely self-contained and autonomous. Of course, this self-definition derived from its determination not to become institutionalized, just another denomination. But it resulted in congregations that drew clear boundaries between themselves and surrounding congregations, whether of other Brethren or of 'the sects' so-called. Such isolation is, of course, incompatible with the principle of the fellowship of all believers. It also fails to resemble the New Testament churches, which were more diverse and flexible than we have given them credit for.

Instead, we have treated the New Testament as a detailed rule book for how assemblies should operate, despite the sparse descriptions of the practices of the early churches.[11] We have, for example, failed to provide an Open Table, even sometimes for Brethren and Sisters from other assemblies, let alone for fellow Christians from other denominations. We have imposed rules of silence and dress codes on female worshippers, thereby limiting the exercise of their spiritual gifts.[12] And we have steadfastly refused to engage in the training and development of leaders and others on the grounds that such organizational planning and structure is the work of Man, not of the Holy Spirit.[13]

As a result of this legalism and conformity, the two features of our movement for which we have been noted—our worship and our evangelism—have both suffered terribly. To quote,

> ...a way of worshipping which was new, fresh, liberating, and exciting 150 years ago [written in 1988] has often become a stale, predictable, rigid, joyless routine.[14]

As for evangelism, much activity is still concerned with a weekly gospel service on Sunday evening, together with occasional evangelistic rallies.

PARTNERSHIP AND ASSOCIATION

These unfortunate trends can be reversed if we put into practice our original principles. If we really are going to be united in our diversity, then we should begin to support other assemblies than our own, and to receive help from them.[15] Furthermore, since we cannot define 'believers' solely in terms of Open Brethren, we should also engage with other denominations and para-church organizations where collaboration would further the Kingdom of God.

The history of Evangelicalism, however, has been one of continuous invention of new sects or movements and new para-church organizations. There are now more than 340 self-styled denominations in the UK alone! We Brethren have ourselves, sadly, been responsible for some of this needless proliferation, particularly in the early stages of our history. Instead of differentiating further, we should take advantage of the great diversity of gifts and graces already represented in this huge array of potential partners.

And our collaboration should not be limited to other Evangelical Christians. There may be occasions when we might work together with Christians of other persuasions, or even with other religions.[16] For example, a local issue concerning freedom of worship would concern all people of faith, and together, their voice would sound far stronger than its separate parts.

But looking even more broadly, perhaps we should stop treating all other human spheres of activity as 'this evil world', and be willing to learn from them and work with them when appropriate. In one sense, we already do this, for we consider it an asset that we freely use the gifts of believers whose daily employment gives them skills and knowledge of benefit to other believers.[17] Further, we know that non-Christians are more likely to identify with people who live lives like their own.

We can also benefit from association at a more general level. Instead of treating science—and evolutionary science in particular—as, by definition, hostile, we can recognize the immense potential for good in science and technology.[18] We can come to appreciate that science and religion have different, not competing, aims and methods. Indeed, many of the processes and outcomes of the natural and social sciences are of potential benefit in Christian work.[19] In particular, an understanding of how organizations operate and develop could be crucial if the Brethren are to succeed in making and retaining converts.

ORGANIZATION AND DEVELOPMENT

Given the vision of a revitalized movement and believers, and the mission of fulfilling Christ's great commission, how then should we *organize* ourselves? The first task is to assess honestly and realistically where we are now. The previous section has suggested various weaknesses, and the latest statistics[20] suggest that Open Brethren assemblies are closing down at an alarming rate. Perhaps the most urgent task, therefore, is to see if declining assemblies at risk of closing can turn themselves around before it is too late, and become, instead, revitalized communities of believers.[21] There is, after all, Biblical justification for a concern with struggling Christians—we only have to read Revelation chapters 2 and 3 to see how important all the existing assemblies were to the apostles.

So, how can this difficult turnaround task be achieved? At the very beginning of any such rescue attempt, it may be necessary to defuse existing conflict.[22] Once this painful issue has been honestly addressed, we may turn to the longer-term task. Normally, the change needed in the assembly in question is radical, and larger than it has ever before contemplated making. Moreover, although some agents of change may already exist in the assembly, the fact that little has occurred hitherto suggests that their presence is not sufficient to initiate the major development required. Newcomers may be needed, who have a *vision* for the assembly and can persuade the current believers to grasp it for themselves. Unless they do so, turnaround efforts are doomed.

However, while new vision is a necessary condition for survival and growth, it is not a sufficient one. A variety of *structural* changes may well be required. In the interests of providing believers with consecutive and comprehensive Bible teaching, it may be necessary to employ a minister.[23] If the existing leadership is unwilling to embrace the vision, new leaders may need to be trained and developed to assume the new responsibility.[24] If decision-making has not been transparent, and the assembly as a whole has had little input, processes will need to change. Instead of decisions all being taken by the same small group of elders, teams of believers might be brought together to promote specific areas of activity—for example, youth work, or gospel outreach, or the worship meeting.[25]

Such attempts to save small assemblies are only part of organizational change and development, however. Larger flourishing assemblies are likely to be able to contribute a great deal. Members may be trained and developed not only to help smaller existing assemblies to revive and grow, but also to plant entirely new ones. And the co-ordination of all such efforts requires a degree of organization at regional level,[26] involving para-church organizations as well as assemblies.[27]

But the real issue is not how to enable the Open Brethren and our assemblies to survive. It is to honour our founders by achieving unity in diversity, and so, leading millions more into the Kingdom of God.

Summary
The Brethren are, like all Protestants, children of the Reformation. The two fundamental insights which they brought to the church were the unity of all believers in Christ and the priesthood of all believers. These required, respectively, a willingness to join in fellowship with any true follower of Christ; and a desire to free believers to exercise the spiritual gifts which the Holy Spirit had given them. Unfortunately, the impetus of these inspirational distinctive features were soon lost. Instead, assemblies' attention was focussed inwardly on a legalistic separatism. The time has come for a rediscovery of our heritage. We should welcome the opportunity to collaborate with our evangelical colleagues in the denominations. And we should make sure that we use the gifts of all believers, old and young, Brothers and Sisters.

NOTES

1. Summerton, Neil (2017) The Reformation and Apologetics. *Partnership Perspectives,* Autumn.
2. Dickson, Neil (2017) The Reformation Now. *Partnership Perspectives,* Autumn.
3. Lane, Tony (1987) Essential and Non-essential Doctrines and Practices. *Christian Brethren Review*, vol. 38.
4. 'Sosthenes' (1977) Sola Scriptura. *Christian Brethren Research Fellowship Journal*, vol. 14.
5. Tinder, Donald (1971) The Brethren Movement in the World Today. Lecture delivered at Granville Chapel, Vancouver, B.C. Found at www.biblicalstudies.org.uk
6. Thomas, Andy (2016) What's New and Special about 'Missional Church'? *Partnership Perspectives,* Autumn.
7. Summerton, Neil (2012) The 'Big Society', Integral Mission, and Social Action: Some Reflections and Concerns. *Partnership Perspectives,* Summer.

8. Summerton, Neil (2016) Reflections on Church without Walls. *Partnership Perspectives,* Autumn.

9. Heading, John (1986) Who are the brethren? Bath: Echoes of Service.

10. Cochran, Robert (1971) Why I left the Brethren. *Christian Brethren Research Journal,* vol. 8.

11. Counter, K. (1971) Why I left the Brethren. *Christian Brethren Research Journal,* vol. 8.

12. Christian Brethren Review, vol. 33 *passim.*

13. Christian Brethren Research Fellowship Journal, vol. 30 *passim.*

14. Baigent, John, (1988) Declare His Glory: A fresh look at our congregational worship. *Christian Brethren Review,* vol. 39.

15. Summerton, Neil (2011) The Independence and Interdependence of Congregations. *Partnership Perspectives,* vol. 46, Spring.

16. Christian Brethren Research Fellowship Journal, vol. 23, *passim.*

17. Guy, Joy (1984) An Overview. *Christian Brethren Review,* vol. 35.

18. Christian Brethren Research Fellowship Journal, vols. 18 & 19, *passim.*

19. Christian Brethren Review, vol. 35, *passim.*

20. Brierley, Peter (2015) Independent churches – how are they doing? *Partnership Perspectives,* vol. 54, Autumn.

21. Summerton, Neil (2016) Turning Churches Round. *Partnership Perspectives,* vol. 57, Summer.

22. Christian Brethren Review, vol. 38, *passim.*

23. Christian Brethren Research Fellowship Journal, vol. 14, *passim.*

24. Clarkson, David, & McQuoid, Stephen (2013) Learning to Lead: Next Generation. OPAL Trust.

25. Hornal, Alistair (2014) Post-Brethrenism and Apostolic Teams. *Partnership Perspectives,* vol. 52, Spring.

26. Summerton, Neil (2015) Editorial. *Partnership Perspectives,* vol. 54, Autumn.

27. Summerton, Neil (2016) Editorial. *Partnership Perspectives,* vol. 55, Autumn.

CHAPTER 4

The Historian's Tale

AN IDEALISTIC MOVEMENT

There is relatively little historical evidence extant regarding the Brethren. For the best available historical scholarship, consult the authoritative *'Gathering to his Name'* by Tim Grass.[1] However, my purpose here is merely to provide a brief historical outline.

Immediately, we are faced with the problem of deciding what should be its fundamental organizing principle. Should we simply put key events in the order in which they occurred? But this begs the question of how to decide which events are key. Should we examine the Brethren from the perspective of church history, then? Clearly, the Brethren have constituted a small but influential element within Protestant Christianity. However, their development has extended far beyond the religious context, as has its outcomes. What about their considerable contribution to theology—in particular, to biblical scholarship? Again, this is an important perspective, but restricted in its interest only to amateur and professional academics.

None of these perspectives can properly serve as a unifying principle for an historical account. The most appropriate approach is to treat the Brethren as a *social movement*. This provides both a sequential rationale for the account, and also some explanations of their continuing history.

Any social movement concentrates upon the achievement of one or a very few aims. Its followers want to change the existing state of affairs for the better. The Brethren movement, which emerged in the late 1820s in Dublin, Ireland, and the West Country of England, was no exception. It was certainly of its own time, for the later eighteenth and early nineteenth centuries were a period of radical religious, political, and economic change. The Industrial Revolution with its concomitant urbanization, the radical and violent French Revolution, and the Methodists' recent urgent appeal to the working class, all provided a vivid backdrop. Radical change was in the air.

So, what was the movement's aim? The Brethren wanted, first, to demonstrate in practice the *unity of all Christian believers*.[2] Such a demonstration required believers to worship and enjoy fellowship freely with one another, regardless of the rules and practices of any denominations to which they might belong.

A second and related aim was to provide the opportunity for all believers to exercise the talents and graces with which God's Holy Spirit has endowed them. This principle of the *'priesthood of all believers'* assumed that their gifts for worship, teaching, and preaching enabled believers to perform these functions without the need for an ordained clergy.

Such free and spontaneous participation was facilitated by the *primitive simplicity* of their religious practice. This avoided ritual and sought to return to the practices of the first Christian churches as described in the New Testament. This third distinctive feature was clearly derived from a fourth: a particularly strong version of the Reformation principle of *sola scriptura*. The Reformers had treated the Bible as the final authority with respect to doctrine and practice—what to believe and how to behave. Brethren insisted that believers should not merely avoid practices that the Bible forbids; they should also reject those that are not expressly enjoined by the apostles or described as having occurred. Since the practices of the New Testament churches are not described in detail, the range of Brethren church activity was limited.

A fifth and final distinctive feature was the idea of *mission 'in faith'*. That is, Brethren were encouraged to respond to Christ's 'great commission' to preach the gospel and gain converts by becoming missionaries, but without drawing a guaranteed salary from a missionary society. They were to rely, instead, on donations from the congregation that had sponsored them. One of the founders of the movement, Anthony Norris Groves, heroically did just this.

There were other central features of Brethren beliefs, values, and practices that were not, however, distinctive. This is because they shared them with other Evangelical Christians from several denominations. The four key elements of Evangelicalism are: a strong emphasis on the event of conversion; an insistence on the working out of the faith in active witness;

a reliance on the Bible as supremely authoritative; and a devotion to the doctrine of the substitutionary atonement, whereby Christ is understood to have been punished in our place to atone for our sins.[3] The Brethren and large swathes of the mainstream churches took these for granted.

Nevertheless, the Brethren distinctives were sufficient to attract large numbers of such Christians to join them over the next 20 years, with some 200 assemblies being formed by 1840.[4] Movements inspire great enthusiasm and effort, since they provide a few clear aims and allow the exercise of personal agency and initiative in the absence of institutional structures and rules. The originators of the Brethren movement were devout and visionary people from educated and often clerical backgrounds. They were ideally suited to propel their movement into prominence. Yet, their idealistic heavenly vision was soon compromised by their all too earthly human nature. And they themselves were responsible for the debacle.

From Movement to Sects

In 1848, leading Brethren disagreed, among other things, about a theological aspect of biblical prophecy regarding the millennium (Christ's thousand-year rule on earth). This disagreement resulted in some assemblies being unwilling to have fellowship with members of others, a blatant contradiction of the first principle of the movement—the fellowship of all believers. Belief was now being taken to constitute acceptance of one particular interpretation of a notoriously difficult part of the Bible, rather than the acceptance of the Evangelical Christian faith.

Two sects emerged from this debacle—the Exclusive and the Open Brethren. The Exclusive Brethren, led by J.N. Darby, subsequently split into sub-sects, the largest of which now merits the label of cult.[5] This is because it is tightly and secretively controlled by a leader who attributes to himself apostolic authority and exercises his power unilaterally by means of punishment by social exclusion.

The Open Brethren, on the other hand, like other sects, started to define themselves negatively in terms of who they were not, rather than retaining their emphasis on the positive aims that they had espoused 20 years before. They now emphasized the *independence of each assembly*[6] as a self-governing congregation (as opposed to the Exclusives, who promoted a central control of doctrine and practice). Instead of acknowledging their Evangelical roots, they started to call Christian denominations 'sects', implying that they themselves were the only true church. The denominations were the creations of sinful Man, whereas they themselves were guided by the Holy Spirit alone. *Absolute separation* from such apostates was required.

This spiritual purity was reinforced by their emphasis on a particular version of biblical prophecy—*dispensational premillennialism*.[7] Premillennialism located them, as the true church, firmly in the spiritual realm, as opposed to the sinful earthly one. Christ, they proclaimed, would soon return to rapture them away with Him into heaven, far from this evil world. Finally, their strong version of *sola scriptura* led them to concern themselves deeply with matters of internal *church order and discipline*. This tendency towards conformity they derived from St Paul's admonitions in his letters to the early churches. It is clearly opposed to the emphases on freedom and spontaneity of worship and on mission to the world espoused by the original Brethren movement (and also, of course, justified by reference to the Bible).

However, these separatist features, derived from the splitting of the movement into sects, did not entirely obscure the original distinctives of the movement. On the contrary, the movement's emphases on mission, fellowship, and spiritual gifts retained enough traction to gradually ease the Open Brethren sect into the status of a quasi-denomination. It was as though the original movement legacy was successful, at least for a time, in limiting the sectarian separatist project.

From Sect to 'Denomination'

The Open Brethren in the UK generally either expanded or held steady in their numbers during the later nineteenth and the first half of the twentieth century,[8] before declining thereafter.[9,10] In the absence of regularly recorded statistics at assembly level, it is plausible to estimate the number of adherents in the UK at somewhere between 50,000 and 100,000. Such numbers necessarily required some considerable *organization* if the Brethren prospectus was to be fulfilled. If missionaries were to be sent across the world, the projects had to be coordinated so that effort was not duplicated. If Brethren were to maintain a modicum of agreement across assemblies in terms of doctrine and practice, then teaching should be provided by a core of itinerant teachers. Likewise, if the Great Commission was going to be fulfilled, a similar core of evangelists was needed. And it would be wasteful of the work of these full-time preachers if their audiences were limited to one assembly at a time: conferences of neighbouring assemblies should be arranged.

These organizational features were supplemented by periodicals containing both information about conferences and other events and also devotional material. Moreover, various assembly needs were met by parachurch organizations: Crusaders, Covenanters, and the Inter-Varsity Fellowship, for example, for youth and student teaching. And Brethren were involved in the major revivalist campaigns run by Evangelicals, where they collaborated with other denominations and benefitted from the additional converts. In sum, no sect of such a size could possibly survive and flourish without organization.

However, this degree of organization clearly violated the distinctives of the sect (while being in accord with those of the original movement from which the sect had sprung). Individuals and assemblies were now collaborating, not just with other assemblies, but even with the denominations. And all sorts of unscriptural things were happening at these conferences and events. Women participated audibly, for example; head covering was conspicuous by its absence; and musical instruments were being used in worship.

A counter-reaction to this degree of organization now reaffirmed the sect's distinctive features at the expense of the movement's, and two opposed narratives—the 'tight' (or conservative) and the 'loose' (or liberal)—gained visibility and supporters.[11] Indeed, the tight Brethren started to describe themselves as a remnant within a remnant.[12] Particular periodicals were associated with the two narratives (e.g. *Precious Seed* vs *Perspectives*), as were organized groupings of assemblies (e.g. Gospel Halls vs Partnership). There were clear geographical and social predictors of allegiance: the tight narrative seemed to be favoured in Northern Ireland, Scotland, and the North of England in rural and small town settings, while the loose one was more popular among middle-class suburban dwellers in the South. There were also differences in numerical strength, which overall was, by now, decreasing. While small rural assemblies were closing down at an alarming rate towards the end of the twentieth century, some large suburban ones were maintaining their numbers or even increasing them.

DIVERSITY AND CONFUSION

But by the second decade of the twenty-first century, the oversimplified description of the Open Brethren in terms of the tight versus loose dichotomy is no longer a tenable account of the situation. It is no longer a matter of defenders of the original movement manifesto versus defenders of its subsequent schismatic sect. Rather, a wide range of congregational types is to be found. There are those who only reluctantly admit to having once been called Brethren, and who now call themselves 'with Brethren roots', or, more brutally, 'ex-Brethren'. There are those, on the other hand, who still refuse to call themselves anything because they hold precious the Assembly Truth that the assembly is the only organization sanctioned by Scripture. And there is every conceivable variant in between.

Some congregations have a salaried and trained professional staff, a website of professional quality, and a variety of missional activities suited to different categories of person. They train members to 'plant' new congregations in surrounding neighbourhoods. Others lobby vigorously against current social developments, which many other Evangelical Christians believe should be challenged on moral grounds. Still more soldier on helping and encouraging each other, believing the biblical injunction that their first duty is towards their fellow saints in the assembly.

This diversity is matched by the increased range and number of parachurch organizations. It reflects the tendency of Evangelicalism constantly to create new groupings and organizations to meet a perceived need or opportunity. When God speaks directly to individual Christians, He tends to give a variety of messages. Nowhere is this more apparent than within Evangelicalism's Charismatic wing, where numerous individuals develop their own 'ministry'—that is, their own organization for evangelism or revival.[13]

It is impossible to predict what the future of the Open Brethren will be amid all this confusion. Fortunately, prediction is not one of the tasks that we historians normally undertake. We are, however, expected to offer some sort of explanation for the developments which we have described, and I will devote the rest of my historical account of the Brethren to this end.

SUCCESS OR FAILURE?

One explanation for the decline of the Brethren in the UK (but not globally[14]) is that it is in the very nature of movements to decline. If they have achieved their aims, there is little need for them to continue. Very often, they succeed by having their aims incorporated into the social system from which they emerged. Or else, they become an institution in their own right, devoted in the long term to ensuring their aims continue to be met. Alternatively, the aims do not remain attractive to enough people to maintain their impetus, and failing to adapt, they simply fade away.

Both of these conclusions might apply to the Open Brethren. Their original movement aims have been recognized and incorporated into Evangelical denominations, which are now much more open to using adherents' aptitudes and knowledge in their missional purpose. And the distinctive features of the subsequent sect—in particular, its authoritarian and conformist character, its isolation, and its strange prophetic beliefs— are unlikely to attract new adherents. While sects are generally unattractive, cults are anathema, so the nominal association of Open *Brethren* with the cultic Taylorite branch of the Exclusive *Brethren* does not help either.

A second possible explanation for Brethren decline lies in the general decline of Christianity in the UK and Europe.[15] Decline of the Brethren may have little to do with the nature of the Brethren as such, but be due merely to the fact that they are a Christian group. Of course, this is no real explanation, but it does at least lead us to explore more general historical and cultural features of the British and European context as possibly implicated in Christianity's decline there. Candidates have been canvassed *ad nauseam*, but most frequently cited are the growth of individualism and consumerism.

To use consumerist language, perhaps there is greater competition in this declining market.[16] Not only is the number of competitors to the Brethren increasing exponentially, but several of them have adopted some of the Brethren distinctives. The House Churches, for example, stress the restoration of original simplicity, but add the attraction of ecstatic Charismatic experiences. The Charismatics permit even their youth to exercise their putative spiritual gifts of healing. And the Anglican Calvinists are so wealthy and well organized that they have exercised a very visible effect on the Church of England's reputation and practice.

Whatever the explanation for the movement's decline in the UK—and those outlined earlier are neither exhaustive nor mutually exclusive—the Brethren offer a fascinating historical insight into the social and religious milieu of modern British society as it hovers on the edge of post-modernity.

Summary

The history of the Brethren is the history of a movement. They are best understood as an idealistic attempt to revive the dominant Evangelicalism from within in early-nineteenth-century Britain. Like many such utopian movements, they soon split into two sects—the Open and the Exclusive Brethren. Typically of sects, they now concentrate more on their differences than on their foundational prospectus. The Open Brethren emphasized the supreme authority of the Bible and the separation of believers from the world. When some of them engaged in evangelistic cooperation with other Christians, and introduced elements of church practice contrary to the Biblical blueprint, open conflict between conservative and liberal factions broke out. The present position is confused, and the prospects for the Open Brethren seem doubtful, at least in the United Kingdom.

NOTES

1. Grass, Tim (2006) Gathering to his Name: The Story of Open Brethren in Britain and Ireland. Milton Keynes: Paternoster.
2. Church Growth Trust (2013) The 'Brethren' movement – a briefing note. Tiverton:Partnership and Oakham: Church Growth Trust.
3. Bebbington, David (1989) Evangelicalism in Modern Britain: A History from the 1730s to the 1980s. London: Unwin Hyman.
4. Grass (op. cit.) p. 61.
5. *The Times,* August 7th, 2017.
6. Summerton, Neil (2011) Reflections on congregational independence, connexionalism, and denominationalism. *Partnership Perspectives,* Spring.
7. Davis, Malcolm (2006) The Christian's Hope. *Believer's Magazine,* November.
8. Grass, op. cit. p. 518.
9. Brown, Graham (2003) Whatever happened to the Brethren? Tiverton: Partnership.
10. Brierley, Peter (2015) Independent churches – how are they doing? *Partnership Perspectives,* Autumn.
11. Grass, op. cit., chapter 20.
12. McBride, Samuel (2008) The local church and its conflict. *Assembly Testimony,* Chapter 12.
13. Herriot, Peter (2016) Warfare and Waves: Calvinists and Charismatics in the Church of England. Eugene, Oregon: Wipf & Stock.
14. Davie, Grace (2002) Europe – The Exceptional Case: Parameters of Faith in the Modern World. London: Darton, Longman, & Todd.
15. Davie, op. cit.
16. Stark, Rodney & Finke, Roger (2000) Acts of Faith: Explaining the Human Side of Religion. Berkeley, California: University of California Press.

CHAPTER 5

The Psychologist's Tale

A CRUCIAL EQUILIBRIUM

Every social system, whether it is religious, political, economic, familial, or whatever, is based on a fundamental principle: the balance between *differentiation* and *integration*.

Differentiation is the system's tendency to distinguish itself from other social systems; integration, to interact with them. Social systems need to differentiate themselves in order to gain participants, since they have to offer something distinctive. They also need to integrate, however, to get the necessary resources acquired through communication and collaboration with other systems.[1]

Each social system oscillates around a point of balance between these two dialectical opposites. The nature of its aims and its current context determine what is its best balance. A clear example is provided by the social institution that is the British monarchy. Clearly, those who constitute the monarchy have to be differentiated from those over whom they, in some sense or other, reign. However, at the same time, they have to demonstrate that they are also—again, in some sense or other—'like us'. As if this were not an almost impossible task, there is the additional complication that the point of equilibrium is changing. As British society becomes increasingly less deferential, this point moves towards the integration pole.

In general, the more sub-systems develop within a global social system, the more differentiated each of these new players will need to be. This is currently the case with both religion and science. Such may be the pressure

© The Author(s) 2018
P. Herriot, *The Open Brethren: A Christian Sect in the Modern World,*
https://doi.org/10.1007/978-3-030-03219-7_5

to differentiate that other methods may be employed to survive and gain members. For example, a sub-system may act in a particularly hostile manner towards its closest competitors in an effort to weaken them or to make them less attractive. It is noteworthy that religious sects are most hostile to those whom they most resemble (and from whom they may have recently acrimoniously separated).

If the sub-system is to clearly demonstrate its distinctive features to potential recruits, it will have to present an unambiguous image. This can only be achieved if its members closely conform to those features, rather than exhibiting a diverse range of behaviour. The more finely differentiated a social system is from others, the more internally conformist it is likely to be.[2]

This scenario is ripe for a familiar psychological process to occur: the formation of prototypes and stereotypes.[3] A prototype is what the ideally conformist member of one's own system is like; a stereotype, the typical member of a rival social system. Conflict between 'us' and 'them' is the likely outcome.

However, all of these ploys may be insufficient to ensure the system's survival. It may decline, and ultimately, fail because it grows too differentiated. It fails to attempt any integration that might redress its imbalance and bring it some support. Or, at the other end of the continuum, it may become so integrated with other systems that it becomes indistinguishable from them and loses its distinctive *raison d'être*.[4]

THE CASE OF THE BRETHREN

The story of the Brethren provides an ideal case study of this dynamic process of movement around an equilibrium. The foundational movement proved popular because it provided differentiating features, which were attractive to many and fitted in well with the religious and general cultural context. At the same time, it maintained its connections with Evangelical Christianity, sharing its key doctrines and its concern for evangelism.

The schism of 1848, however, resulted in the Open Brethren seeking to differentiate themselves from the Exclusives. To this end, they emphasized, in particular, the complete independence and autonomy of each congregation, as opposed to the more central control of the Exclusives. Further, they developed their own terminology, which differentiated them from mainstream denominations. This book is already replete with examples, especially in Chap. 2. For a brief list, see the Glossary on pp. 171.

In order to ensure clear differentiation, they had to maintain a high level of internal conformity of behaviour. Although there was no written constitution or set of rules, informal norms were enforced by social pressure. As a result, their religious and general social practice was uniform, and such visible differentiators as dress and appearance were closely adhered to. While the original emphasis of the movement was on freedom to exercise individual gifts, the post-schism orthodoxy was much more conformist. It stressed the separation and purity of the believer from the world and from the denominations, indicating a wide variety of religious and social behaviours that were disapproved.

The predictable consequence of this authoritarian and conformist approach was conflict, but not this time with the Exclusives. Rather, it was with some elements of the Open Brethren, who began to re-emphasize the original distinctive features of the movement. We should not forget, these non-conformists argued,[5] that our founding principle was the fellowship of all believers. How can we then refuse to have anything to do with our fellow Christians?

Perceiving a threat to the new orthodoxy, its upholders began to abuse these revivers of the original flame. The 'loose' Open Brethren were attacked for feeling that "existing assembly life was too narrow and needed a large input of human organisation", a view propounded by "professionally well qualified academics and business leaders along with certain Bible teachers".[6] This loose perspective "is frankly hostile to the Scriptural truth of the normative pattern of New Testament assembly principles". Indeed, so careless were these well-educated brethren of Scriptural truth that they encouraged feminism and polluted the simplicity of the New Testament Church.[7]

Clearly, a stereotype of the loose Brethren was held by their tight counterparts. They were middle-class, educated people who favoured trendy ideas that were eating away at the foundations of Assembly Truth. They were doomsayers,[8] who failed to give credit to the work of the Holy Spirit in humble Gospel Halls all over the country. Such stereotypes are a likely concomitant of inter-group conflict.

Significantly, the usual response on the part of the loose Brethren was to argue that their opponents were misinterpreting Scripture. The possibility that there might be other criteria for establishing doctrine and practice than the Bible was not entertained—the foundations of conservative Evangelicalism were not to be disturbed, however loose a Brother you were. But the outcome of these disputes was to render it doubly likely that the Open Brethren would decline: the tight faction would become too differentiated, and the loose, too integrated.

Systems and People

From a psychological perspective, however, religious social systems are not of great interest in themselves. What we psychologists are really concerned with is the relationship between the systems and their adherents. How does a particular system affect its adherents, and conversely, how do they affect the system? Do particular types of people create and maintain religious systems, or do systems work by encouraging people to think about themselves in particular ways?

To address the last of these questions first, at least in so far as it refers to fundamentalist movements such as the Brethren, the answer is clear. Numerous attempts have been made to discover personality traits or types that make individuals more likely to find fundamentalism more attractive, and few positive results have been found. The only trait which has been reliably shown to correlate with fundamentalist beliefs and attitudes is *authoritarianism*. This is defined as a higher than average degree of submission to authority, aggression towards out-groups, and conventional social attitudes. Fundamentalist adherents are more likely to be authoritarian, but the direction of causality is not established: they may have become more authoritarian as a result of their adherence, rather than choosing adherence because they were already authoritarian.

A more profitable approach is to explore the development of *social identities*, and the way in which these contribute to the self-concept.[9] A social identity is the belief that one belongs to a specific category of person. It becomes an element of the self-concept when one internalizes the beliefs, values, and practices of that category and treats them as one's own. Identity formation is a continuously negotiated process: the individual experiences pressure from a social system to conform, but may resist on the basis of his or her existing self-concept.[10]

Simple and Complex Identities

Clearly, from the perspective of social identity theory, people are likely to maintain several different social identities at the same time. In the modern world, we operate within a variety of social systems, so we are likely to hold occupational, religious, cultural, and many other identities within our notions of who we are. Hence, it is the variety of, and the relations between, our social identities that help form our self-concept and others' perceptions of us. It is rare indeed that we meet someone whose self is entirely defined by a single social identity.

However, my analysis begins with the single social identity. An identity becomes salient in the social situation in which it is appropriate, and usually guides our behaviour, largely to the exclusion of other identities.[11] If the situation is the Sunday morning Breaking of Bread, the Brethren identity becomes salient, together with a range of practices to undertake (and others to avoid). Other identities are not salient, for example, one's occupational identity, and the norms and practices of the occupational social system are simply irrelevant.

Every simple social identity, by definition, excludes other categories of person, but is not necessarily hostile towards them. However, tight Brethren, for example, are generally hostile to identities based on education, entertainment, politics, the media, and science. Stereotypes of these social systems make it difficult for those with a Brethren identity to internalize identities based upon them, or at the very least, to allow such identities to become prominent.

Indeed, the model of the social world espoused by tight Brethren can actually make it possible to downgrade all other social identities than that of Brethren. This is achieved by lumping together every other social system under the category of 'the world', and then, treating this all-inclusive category as a hostile out-group to be opposed or avoided.[12] The consequence is that Brethren adopt a Brethren mode of behaviour in every social situation.

However, social systems are usually interrelated in a variety of ways: ethnicity and gender, for example (e.g. black women), or nationality and occupation (e.g. Chinese scientists). These systemic relations are often internalized as *'cross-hatched'* social identities,[13] where the category to which one believes oneself to belong is a compound of two apparently unrelated simple categories: Scottish assemblies, for example, or unmarried sisters. Such cross-hatched identities may possibly threaten the identity of Brethren if they become more central to the believer's self-concept than the assembly itself.

Another more complex form of identity is the idea of *'nested'* identity.[14] Here, the instance of a superordinate social system with a variety of subsystems within it becomes represented in the mind as a category subsuming sub-categories. So, the superordinate social identity of Evangelical Christian may subsume a variety of nested identities—for example, Open Brethren, Baptists, Independents, Pentecostals, and so on. The superordinate identity has certain distinctive features common to all Evangelicals, while the nested identities add to these basics the differentiating features of each of the various sub-categories.

Thus, it becomes possible for one situation (for example, a joint gospel mission) to result in the salience of the superordinate Evangelical identity, while another (Sunday morning worship) to prioritize one of the nested identities. And the core Evangelical beliefs will become of primary importance in the first situation, the secondary denominational ones in the second.

Note, however, that the core beliefs are inviolable. The loose Brethren had to justify their collaboration with 'the sects' by arguing the scriptural toss with their tight critics. The latter, for their part, do not entertain nested identities: all scriptural truths apply in every situation, as far as they are concerned. Such a degree of dominance of a single simple social identity is likely to make integration, and hence, the achievement of an equilibrium, impossible. The tight Brethren are likely to decay rapidly as a result.[15]

PSYCHOLOGICAL BENEFITS

Why, then, do people still retain their adherence to such social systems as the Open Brethren? After all, they are hardly noted for their popularity or social standing. The psychological answer is that they meet several fundamental psychological needs.

This is hardly surprising when we consider the nature of social identities. A social identity is internalized into the self-concept. Hence, when the social system that generates this identity is in peril or triumphant, it is individuals themselves who are threatened or successful. The motivational power towards fear or joy and subsequent appropriate behaviour is potentially immense. Tales of persecution are potent motivators.

For a start, the Brethren social identity provides a sure and certain view of the world and of one's own position within it. The narrative runs as follows. God Himself, through His word the Bible, provides the authoritative justification for our world-view—and one cannot have a greater authority than this. The world may thrash around wildly, unaware that its destiny has already been determined by Almighty God. Believers, however, know the secret of much of His plan for the future. They do not know all the details, for example, the precise date of His return to rapture all believers up into heaven. Perhaps in His wisdom He has not revealed it, in order to prevent people taking advantage of the assured interval to gratify their sinful lusts.[16] But believers know for sure the essential features of their own exalted future state, and by way of contrast, the awful fate reserved for unrepentant sinners.

The need for *certainty*[17] is not just met in terms of the cosmic future, however. All uncertainty about what to believe and how to act is removed too, since the Holy Spirit enables believers to interpret the clear meaning of the Scriptures. In a post-modern world where truth and morality are relative concepts, God's Word alone gives confidence and assurance.

Another psychological benefit of a Brethren social identity is enhanced *self-esteem*.[18] Believers have plenty of others with whom to compare themselves favourably. First are the other movements and sects, who deny 'Assembly Truth', the key differentiating features of the Open Brethren. Second are the denominations, dominated by Man-made organization, rather than by the leading of the Holy Spirit alone. And third is 'the world', all other social systems, whose ridicule of them only confirms their virtuous status. After all, since the world is sinful, its disapproval must signal their own purity.

Believers may also think better of themselves as a result of the high status that God has bestowed upon them. True, it is God's undeserved grace by means of which they are saved. But they themselves have had to exercise faith, and take the crucial decision to convert. So, their subsequent spiritual state, superior to that of the carnal world, and their infinite privileges as Christ's bride thereafter, are markers of their exalted standing and true worth.

In addition to enhanced certainty and self-esteem, believers also have their needs for *affiliation*[19] met in the assembly. In a world where there has never been more communication, loneliness is nevertheless a constant threat, and human relationships and a feeling of belonging remain essential to personal well-being.

Now, tight Brethren have differentiated themselves markedly from external social systems and erected barriers against them. Further, they have sought to bring about a degree of conformity of beliefs, values, and practices within the assembly. Consequently, the assembly comes to constitute a social microcosm, a body of people who are different from external others, and therefore, difficult for these others to form relationships with. However, adherents are similar—and therefore, attractive—to each other. Since the assembly constitutes the major source of personal relationships, it becomes the individual believer's predominant means of meeting their affiliative needs. While some converts may give up many rewarding 'worldly ties', others may find more satisfying relationships within the assembly than they enjoyed before. And those 'born into' the Brethren will never have known anything different.

INFINITE COMPLEXITY

Both at the individual psychological level and at the level of social systems, this account has been drastically over-simplified. I have hardly scratched at the surface of why separation and purity, or authority and conformity, are so powerfully attractive to so many. Nor have I done justice to the dynamic nature of identity formation, in which parties send details of the identity they expect an individual to embrace, and the recipient of the message responds in terms of the extent they are prepared to accept. In particular, I have omitted hitherto the inequalities of *power*[20] so often evident in this exchange.

To remedy this latter omission briefly, let us suppose converts to Evangelical Christianity, converted in a mission, arrive at an assembly. They are entirely at a loss as to what behaviour is expected of them, and so, it is easy for an assembly elder to ensure compliant belief and conduct. Further, in the absence of any higher human authority than the assembly elders, this usually self-appointed body of older men can exercise relatively unchecked power. Faced with such overwhelming odds, any dissenters leave rather than try to negotiate a less exclusive identity.

There is, of course, a huge chasm between this reality of an authoritarian gerontocracy and the rhetoric of the priesthood of all believers. To use a political analogy, it is reminiscent of utopian anarchy so easily morphing into communist tyranny. Any such visible gap between prospectus and lived experience is, as history has repeatedly demonstrated, impossible to contain.

Finally, I should stress that the social systems under discussion in this chapter are, from a global social perspective, a tiny sub-set. Open Brethren are a sub-system of Evangelical Christianity, which is a sub-system of Christianity, which is a sub-system of religion, which, together with science, government, business, media, the arts, and others, is a global sub-system of the global social system.[21] Thus, the social identity of Open Brother nested within Evangelical Christianity is a mental representation of only a tiny part of the global social system. Complex late-modern identities are likely to be nested within much larger super-ordinate categories, ultimately that of humankind, the entire global social system. For many people today experience the sharing of a common fate with the rest of humankind; their super-ordinate identity is that of a human being.

Summary
Like any other social system, the Open Brethren have to achieve a balance between differentiating themselves from others and integrating with them in order to benefit from their resources. Because they are a sect, they have concentrated on the differences in their beliefs and practices from those of similar sects. They ensure conformity within the sect so that it may be clear to others in what respects they are different. As a result, they have a strong social identity as Brethren, which meets their needs for meaning and certainty, self-esteem, and affiliation. However, the centrality of this identity for their self-concept has two results. First, they tend to regard other categories of person as out-groups to be avoided; and second, they may miss out on more complex forms of social identity, which are necessary to function socially in the complex modern world.

NOTES

1. Brewer, Marilynn (2009) Motivations underlying ingroup identification: Optimal distinctiveness and beyond. In Sabine Otten, Kai Sassenberg, and Thomas Kessler (eds) Intergroup Relations: The Role of Motivation and Emotion. Hove: Psychology Press.
2. Hogg, Michael & Abrams, Dominic (2003) Intergroup behaviour and social identity. In Michael Hogg & Joel Cooper (eds) Handbook of Social Psychology. London: Sage.
3. Wright, Steven, & Taylor, Donald (2003) The social psychology of cultural diversity: Social stereotyping, prejudice, and discrimination. In Michael Hogg & Joel Cooper (eds) Handbook of Social Psychology: London: Sage.
4. Taves, Ann (2009) Religious Experience Reconsidered, ch. 1. Princeton, New Jersey: Princeton University Press.
5. Summerton, Neil (2011) Reflections on congregational independence, connexionalism, and denominationalism. *Partnership Perspectives*, Spring.
6. McBride, Samuel (2008) Chapter 12: The local church and its conflict. In Book 3: The Glory of the Local Church. *Assembly Testimony Magazine*.
7. Editorial (1993): Assemblies under pressure to change. *Assembly Testimony Magazine*, November/December.
8. Editorial (2003) *Precious Seed*, vol. 58, no. 4.
9. Cote, James & Levine, Charles (2002) Identity Formation, Agency, and Culture, ch. 2. Mahwah, New Jersey: Lawrence Erlbaum.
10. Jenkins, Richard (2008) Social Identity (3rd edn). London: Routledge.

11. Tajfel, Henri, & Turner, John (1986) The social identity theory of inter-group behaviour. In Steven Worchel & W. G. Austin (eds) Psychology of Intergroup Relations. Chicago: Nelson-Hall.
12. Davis, Malcolm (1990) The Christian and the world. *Precious Seed,* vol. 41, no. 5.
13. Brewer, Marilynne, op. cit.
14. Vescio, Theresa, Hewstone, Miles, Crisp, Richard & Rubin, J. Mark (1999) Perceiving and responding to multiply categorizable individuals: Cognitive processes and affective intergroup bias. In Dominic Abrams & Michael Hogg (eds) Social Identity and Social Cognition. Oxford: Blackwell.
15. Davies, Phil (2014) Are we in the final decade of Open Brethren churches in Wales? *Partnership Perspectives,* Spring.
16. Coles, Howard (2000) Why doesn't the Bible tell us exactly when the Lord will return? *Precious Seed,* vol. 55, no. 1.
17. Hogg, Michael (2006) Self-conceptual uncertainty and the lure of belonging. In Rupert Brown & Dora Capozza (eds) Social Identities: Motivational, Emotional, and Cultural Influences. Hove: Psychology Press.
18. Long, K. & Spears, R. (1997) The self-esteem hypothesis revisited: Differentiation and the disaffected. In R. Spears, P.J. Oakes, N. Ellemers & S.A. Haslam (eds) The Social Psychology of Stereotyping and Group Life. Oxford: Blackwell.
19. Fitness, Julie, Fletcher, Garth, & Overall, Nickola (2003) Interpersonal attraction and intimate relationships. In Michael Hogg & Joel Cooper (eds) Handbook of Social Psychology. London: Sage.
20. Jenkins, op. cit.
21. Beyer, Peter (2006) Religions in Global Society. London: Routledge.

CHAPTER 6

Brethren Lives

Roots

The four narratives I have sketched out so far are my attempts to bring together the public writings of groups of people who represent different perspectives on the Brethren. The second and third chapters are sourced mostly from magazines written by Brethren themselves, which express, respectively, tight and loose narratives. Chapters 4 and 5 present more of an outsider's perspective, the historical Chap. 4 making use of a considerable body of academic work while the psychological Chap. 5 applies to the Brethren well-established theories from social psychology.

All of these narratives, however, may feel removed from the experience of ordinary tight Brethren, who are not, in general, given to committing their beliefs, values, and daily activities to print or social media. How can we access what their allegiance means to them in their daily lives? What, in short, does an ordinary Brethren life look like? One source of such an insight is provided by the regular obituary column of one of the tight Brethren magazines, the *Believer's Magazine*, entitled 'With Christ'.

This monthly record of the completed lives of ordinary adherents consists of edited submissions by readers. The editing frequently requires the reduction in length of the obituaries submitted. We can assume that these accounts reflect the views of readers about how an ordinary Brethren life is best described and understood. The analysis is based on the obituaries of 469 Brothers and Sisters published between May 2012 and May 2017.

© The Author(s) 2018
P. Herriot, *The Open Brethren: A Christian Sect in the Modern World*,
https://doi.org/10.1007/978-3-030-03219-7_6

The first obvious characteristic of these recently deceased adherents is that they are almost all locals rather than cosmopolitans,[1] or to use the title of a recent popular commentary, they are 'Somewheres' rather than 'Anywheres'.[2] These are people with deep local roots, who identify with a particular place and culture. Even if they have moved abroad, many return to the place of their birth in their retirement. Indeed, a high proportion (43 per cent) is recorded as having remained in one assembly for more than 40 years. Locals are likely to mistrust cosmopolitan ideas and life-styles, and may have suffered unfortunate outcomes from globalization.

The readership of the *Believer's Magazine* is primarily located in Northern Ireland and Scotland, with 62 per cent of the deceased dying in the former country and 31 per cent in the latter. Many of the tight Brethren assemblies in Northern Ireland are located in villages or market towns where farming is a major sector of employment. In Scotland, they are to be found predominantly in the central industrial belt and in once thriving centres of the mining and fishing industries.

The long lives of many of the deceased have been harsh indeed. With an average age at death of 83, most had experienced World War II. When family tragedies were added to the dangers and insecurities of their work-ing lives, these men and women had to call on all their reserves of courage and resilience. In all the following quotations, I have substituted initials for full names.

> "S had a difficult life, firstly in managing a small farm and caring for their two young children while T was hospitalised for many months in Belfast. Later she had to come to terms, not only with the homecall of her husband, but also with the untimely death of her step-brother, murdered by terrorists. She was predeceased by her son and daughter, both dying when middle-aged. In spite of all her hardships, S's faith never wavered" (and she died at 96!).

Some hardships were voluntarily undertaken for the sake of the assem-blies. Consider, for example, the situation of the wife of a travelling evangelist:

> They began married life in Londonderry, where J was the manager of a shoe shop, but soon after he was called of God to full-time service as an evange-list. In effect both of them were called, as J could not have done what he did without the wholehearted support of his wife. E willingly and without com-plaint was left at home, sometimes for months at a time, looking after and bringing up their two daughters, M and M. Sometimes she was both mother

and father to them, making toys and playing games, as well as doing whatever jobs needed to be done around the house – baking, cooking and sewing along with cutting firewood, painting fences, and minor repair work.

In the rest of this chapter, I will describe how the life courses of the deceased were charted in their obituaries almost entirely in terms of their *relationship with the assembly*. We must, of course, bear in mind that the obituaries were submitted to a religious magazine, not, for example, to a local newspaper. They follow a predictable sequence: first, potential adherents had to be *accredited*, that is, admitted into the assembly. This always required a specific prior conversion event. Next, they showed themselves *faithful*, at the least by attending meetings regularly when not ill. A few were 'full-time in the work', answering a further specific *vocational* call to preach at home or abroad while relying on the assembly for financial support. Most, however, demonstrated their faithfulness in other forms of service. When they passed away, they were accorded esteem and *respect*, especially at their funeral. They were then understood to be *translated* to a much better place with Christ.

ACCREDITATION

Most Brethren and Sisters were brought up in 'godly' homes, many Brethren but some Methodist, Baptist, and so on. However, there was no suggestion that they might have imbibed the faith together with their mother's milk. They too, like anyone else, had to undergo a single specific conversion experience in which they consciously accepted the substitutionary sacrifice of Christ on the cross for their sins. I myself was brought before the elders (one of whom was my father) to give an account of my conversion, prior to my baptism and reception into fellowship. To their credit, they did not continue to insist on me recounting a specific occasion after I had told them I could not remember ever not being a Christian.

However, this is certainly not normally the case with the deceased. I could not discover more than 10 per cent of the 469 obituaries when a conversion event was not mentioned. A typical account specifies the date of their conversion (or at least, their age); the place; the name of the preacher; the verse of Scripture by which they were convicted of their personal sin and the means of salvation; and finally, the relief of their troubled soul as a consequence. Here is a typical example:

> W was saved as a boy of 15, I Corinthians 15.3 being the Scripture used by the Spirit to bring peace to his troubled soul. His conversion took place during the 10th week of meetings in Shanaghan Gospel Hall conducted by WB. Shortly after his conversion, he was baptised and received into fellowship at Shanaghan.

Where someone had been converted in another denomination, they are described as being led, either by the Bible or by a Brother or Sister, to realize that believer's baptism (by immersion) and then assembly fellowship was the only true New Testament model for the church. This was, as it were, a two-stage process, with conversion to the faith being later followed by the acceptance of 'Assembly Truth'. To quote:

> M's parents were Methodists and he was a regular church attender. When he was 16, the Methodist Chapel convened a series of gospel meetings, and as M attended these meetings, he discovered he was a guilty sinner in need of God's salvation if he was ever to get to Heaven. It was during these meetings that M trusted Jesus Christ for salvation. The night after his conversion, the gospel preacher invited M to his home and gave him a Bible and the good advice 'Read your Bible every day and pray every day'. As he grew and progressed in the reading of the Scripture, M learned new truths and realized that many of the Scripture teachings were not taught in Methodism. As a result of this, he felt he had to find those who were committed to following the Word of God.

The old-fashioned conversion from a life of flagrant sin, a favourite narrative of gospel preachers, did not feature often in these obituaries. When it did, however, florid details were the order of the day. For example:

> B in early life was gripped by the power of alcohol for many years, often lying out in haysheds hopelessly drunk, but on 10th January, 1968 the power of God delivered him and saved him. B had been attending meetings at Tandragee (Co Armagh) when the preachers were SM and GM. A friend....... had taken B in to his home. That night B began to sing; they thought he was drunk, but it was a new song of deliverance – Psalm 40.3.

Whatever the details of their conversion, from the new believer's perspective, the rapid sequence of conversion, baptism, and reception into the assembly was the turning point of their life, the beginning of their 'new life in Christ'. There was a sharp distinction between the old and the new, the sinful 'then' and the saved 'now'. There was the series of very public acts of commitment;

a new set of mentors willing to befriend and guide; and a new social status and central social identity. All of these changes made it very difficult to reconsider one's decision. The die was cast; there was no going back.

So ran the conversion narrative. In fact, the change of lifestyle and behaviour was probably not particularly radical for those who had been 'brought up in a godly family'. But as far as the Brethren are concerned, the recruitment of new Brothers and Sisters is crucial. For assemblies, like other religious bodies, cannot survive if their religious rituals (in their case the Breaking of Bread, the prayer meeting, the Bible reading, the ministry meeting, and the preaching of the gospel) are not carried on. And these rituals need, to put it bluntly, bums on pews.

FAITHFULNESS

Hence the importance of faithfulness and consistency. 'Faithful', referring primarily to attendance at meetings, is the single most frequent adjective or adverb used in the obituaries, both for deceased Brothers and for Sisters. The attendance of both Brothers and Sisters is vital for the maintenance of the assembly. Otherwise, worship cannot go on, unlike elsewhere, where the priest can continue faithfully offering up Holy Mass in an empty church.

The five descriptors in decreasing order of frequency after 'faithful' were, for Brothers, 'consistent', 'quiet', 'loving', 'respected', and 'active'. For Sisters, the sequence is 'hospitable', 'consistent', 'quiet', 'interested', and 'godly'. There is one adjective used of several Brothers but not of a single Sister—'able'. Conversely, quite a few Sisters are described as 'meek', but no Brothers whatsoever.

Evidently, the gender roles mandated by the Brethren are followed in a Brethren life well lived. Men are in control as overseers of the assembly and correspondents on its behalf. They do the important spiritual work of evangelism and teaching, or else carry out traditional manly physical tasks. Women support the men (as 'helpmeets'), but also provide comfort and help to all those who need them.

We should note, however, that even within these gendered parameters, there is a varied set of gifts in demand. Among those tasks which keep the assembly functioning and feature in the obituaries are the following: precentor (leading the singing), visiting the sick and elderly, teaching Sunday School, knitting and praying for missionaries, handing out leaflets, maintaining and cleaning the Gospel Hall, welcoming worshippers as they enter, entertaining visiting preachers in one's home, and above all, one-to-one personal evangelism or 'witnessing'.

So central is this responsibility that when I returned to the hospital treating my father to discover that he had died overnight at an advanced age, the nurse told me that during the night, he had sought to introduce her to his Saviour, which, she remarked, was very sweet of him. A Scottish Sister's obituary describes how she was so zealous in her witnessing that new students at the local university were advised in the university's welcoming literature that she was likely to approach them and ask them if they were saved.

The result of the multiplicity of roles available is that many Brothers and Sisters feel they have a wide range of tasks to undertake for which they are respected and valued. It is not surprising that one obituary reads: "As a person, W had few interests apart from his Lord, his family, and his church".

VOCATION

Without doubt, however, the highest status is bestowed on those who are 'full-time in the work'. Brothers who are evangelists or ministers of the Word are honoured, for they win souls for the Lord (and for the assembly), or build up the saints in their faith and understanding of God's Word. Their obituaries are notably longer than those of the other deceased, and their wives are praised for their support for the demanding task (particularly given the frequent absences of their husbands 'on the road'). The following two obituaries give a feel for the high esteem in which such brethren are held. After all, they provide the ideological glue which keeps the Brethren at least somewhat similar in belief and practice across the different assemblies.

> He was much appreciated in the local assembly and laboured widely in Scotland. In the local assembly his exhortations on a Lord's Day morning were refreshing. There are many in assembly fellowship today who came to know the Lord Jesus Christ through his preaching. One of his favourite expressions was 'It is good to be saved', and the words of the Apostle Paul could be ascribed to J: 'I have fought a good fight, I have finished my course'. Even in declining health his conviction was always in the things of the Lord Jesus Christ. He had an interest in all who attended to him, and took an opportunity to pass on a word in season to them. One desire was that he could preach one more gospel message.

And again:

> A put his heart into evangelising through preaching and visitation, having a pleasing personality. He led the singing in the large conferences in Belfast for 40 years.......He partnered with a number of brethren, but for the

greater part with the late JH and latterly with JR. The Lord richly blessed
the work over the years, and many souls were saved and added to the assemblies......A was faithful to the Word of God, declaring the whole counsel of
God simply and clearly. He loved to preach in the open air........He was
called upon to conduct many Christian weddings and funeral services which
he did with great dignity.

But the biggest heroes are the missionaries, whose lives are often characterized by hardship, danger, and unpredictability. Here is one account:

In her teenage years, S became interested in missionary work, and, when
aged 18, she enrolled in a nursing course at Ballochmyle Hospital and joined
with other young men and women (known as the Ballochmyle seven) who
also had a burning desire to serve God in foreign fields. RR was one of
them, and a relationship started which spanned 54 years and two continents
in the service of God. They were married in 1961 and had 54 wonderful
years together, 49 of which were in the Lord's work. They were blessed with
three of a family [sic], C, J, and N. Their original intention was to go to
India.......At the last minute their visas were cancelled, so preventing them
from travelling. This was a serious blow and they were much cast upon the
Lord who soon indicated His clear direction in the prayer of a brother quoting 'from India even unto Ethiopia' from Esther 1.1..........New plans were
made and they travelled out to Ethiopia to serve the Lord in 1969, believing
they would be there for many years........Sadly, in 1973, a communist government came to power. The Rs found it impossible to continue working in
Ethiopia and they left with all the other missionaries in 1978. After the communist government was overthrown in 1991, R and S returned to Ethiopia
in 1993 to find that the assembly in Addis Ababa, around 30-strong in
1978, had grown to over 300 believers.

[The Rs continued to visit Ethiopia for a quarter of the year to give Bible
teaching to this first-generation church. R spent the rest of the time as an
itinerant evangelist in the UK, "doing pioneer work in the portable hall,
ever supported by S, who was behind him all the way" before she died in
2015].

Of course, many missionaries are Sisters. When they go out to the mission field with their husbands, their role seems little different from that of
the Sisters at home, but with added hardships and uncertainty. However,
when they serve as single women, they are often responsible for the work.
Many go as qualified nurses or teachers, as did one of my own aunts and
two of my female cousins. They served in Africa or India for the entire
course of their working lives.

RESPECT

Although there is, without doubt, a status hierarchy in the Brethren, every Brother and Sister can be treated with respect for their own contribution. Funerals are a major vehicle for the public paying of respect. At most Brethren funerals, there is more than one service, for example, at the home, at the grave side, and in the Gospel Hall. These are normally addressed by one or more Brothers who are 'full-time in the work'. They are distinguished in the obituary notice from 'local brethren', who usually perform assistant roles. The numbers attending are noted, and treated as an indication of the high esteem in which the deceased was held.

Attenders are differentiated into the saved and the unsaved, the latter often family or neighbours. A gospel message is usually preached so that the unsaved are exposed to its challenge, and prayers are solicited from the readers of the obituary that the unsaved will be brought to the Lord as a result. Little did many of these 'unsaved' mourners expect to be the target of attempts to convert them. In fact, none of the 469 obituaries indicated that the deceased had been saved at a funeral.

Here are typical accounts of funerals:

> Her funeral, which was one of the largest ever seen in the district, was conducted by JW in the home, and by AG and RP in the hall and at the graveside, where many who would not often be in meetings heard the gospel faithfully preached. Prayer would be appreciated for her husband, her son and daughter and family circle at Portadown, and her three brothers.

> Her large funeral service from Glengormley Gospel Hall was shared by TM, WM, IG, and AK, and was attended not only by many assembly believers but also by her former neighbours and work colleagues before whom she had borne a good and faithful testimony. Prayer valued for those in the family circle not saved yet.

TRANSLATION

Like conversions, funerals are a major signifier in a Brethren life. They perform the usual functions, but additionally have two further advantages. The first is that the local community cannot but help notice the care and esteem with which Brethren treat their adherents. And second, the immensity of the difference between this earthly life and the heavenly life to come is emphasized.

The labours and sorrows of this life, which are a harsh reality for many of these believers, are replaced by translation into the presence of their beloved Lord. Some of the following phrases may seem sentimental, but they serve to point to the eternal spiritual reward which Brethren believe they will enjoy. They particularly highlight the adoration of the person of Christ, which is at the centre of their most important service, the Breaking of Bread.

> Her health was poor in recent days, but for BS it is now far better – she is with the Lord she loved in that place in His Father's house he has prepared for her.

> When the Lord called him home suddenly, while it was a great shock for the family, for him it was 'absent from the body and present with the Lord'.

> H had arranged the funeral and thanksgiving services herself, and at the close her favourite hymn was sung heartily in a packed hall: 'When He takes me by the hand, And leads me to the promised land, What a day, glorious day, that will be'.

> The toils, tears and trials of her life have been replaced with 'pleasures for evermore'. (Ps 16.11)

Assembly and Believer

These obituary notices point to the intimate relationship between the social system of the assembly and the social identity of the believer. The local roots of many believers help to explain why their now insecure place in a changing world may have attracted them to the certainties of the assembly. For the old identities derived from working at a skilled job in a flourishing local industry are now seldom available.

The new Brethren identity has to become central to the self-concept of converts if they are to become faithful adherents. This being so, the accreditation process requires previous identities to be discarded or downgraded. The association of conversion with rapid induction into assembly fellowship provides a secure environment for this personal change to occur. Faced with the unfamiliar social situation of the assembly, the convert is amenable to internalizing the beliefs, values, and norms of behaviour associated with the new social identity.

Faithfulness and consistency are the key values, with reliable attendance ensuring the continuance of the assembly, provided that those with the more public spiritual gifts exercise them. Plenty of opportunities for the exercise of preaching or leadership gifts will occur, but many other roles are also available in the assembly. For recent converts, these opportunities to become a valued part of the assembly community provide a more than adequate replacement for discarded previous social identities.

The obituaries bookend the beginning and end of the life course. They mark the entry into the only truly pure and simple church of God, that is, the Brethren, and departure thence into the blinding heavenly reality of which even the Brethren are but a dim shadow. The identity of faithful saint, rewarding as it is, is nothing compared with the glory that is to follow.

In sum, the ongoing cycle of assembly practice provides certainty and meaning, self-esteem and confidence, and fellowship and affiliation to adherents. This is a major reason why such a counter-cultural sect continues to survive.

Summary

A study of obituary notices indicates that there is a typical narrative pattern for a Brethren life. The narrative is almost entirely couched in spiritual terms. The Brother or Sister is converted on a specific occasion, an event which is treated as the turning point in their lives. Shortly after, they are baptized and received into assembly fellowship. They then come to perform roles within the assembly, depending on the gifts bestowed upon them by the Holy Spirit, and on their gender. A wide range of roles is available, but the most fundamental virtue is faithfulness, that is, regular attendance. Their life in the assembly is treated as a pale reflection of the glory and peace that is to be enjoyed when they are taken to meet their Lord in heaven. Their funerals celebrate this joyful release from their earthly burdens and show to the wider community the esteem with which they are held in the assembly.

NOTES

1. Gouldner, Alvin (1957) Cosmopolitans and locals: Toward an analysis of latent social roles. *Administrative Science Quarterly*, 2, 281–306.
2. Goodhart, David (2017) The Road to Somewhere: The New Tribes Shaping British Politics. London: Penguin.

CHAPTER 7

Salvation and Service

Testimonies

Brethren obituaries provide a fruitful source for understanding the general narrative of the lives of ordinary Brethren and Sisters. Even in these general accounts, however, conversion to the faith and fellowship with the assembly stood out as landmarks in the story. So vital was 'getting saved' for the rest of the narrative to be told that even in brief obituary notices, an astonishing degree of detail was provided. These details, however, were factual in nature: date, place, preacher, and so on. We learn little about the personal experience of conversion.

This disadvantage is not present in the evidence used for this chapter, however, which consists of the testimonies of Brethren who are 'full-time in the work', either within their own country or abroad on the mission field. These esteemed Brethren wrote a series of articles in the tight Brethren magazine *Assembly Testimony* entitled "My conversion and call". The articles which I have reviewed span ten years' issues of the magazine, from 1997 to 2006, when they were discontinued. Like the obituaries, the sample is taken from the most recent issues of the magazines available, providing a perspective on the tight Brethren narrative which is as contemporary as possible.

All the articles within this period were analysed, apart from two which did not meet the requirements of their title. There remain 58 accounts, all written by men, despite the fact that many single Sisters served as missionaries. They provide arresting insights into the details of Brethren lives and

© The Author(s) 2018   59
P. Herriot, *The Open Brethren: A Christian Sect in the Modern World*,
https://doi.org/10.1007/978-3-030-03219-7_7

experiences, and their relationship to the assemblies. What, we may wonder, was the family background of these eminent Brethren, and how did it affect their lives? What was their reported experience of conversion? What was the nature of their call to their full-time ministry, and how were they formed and prepared for it? What effect did their formation have on their attitudes to their work and family lives, in particular on their relationships with their wife and children? And most important, what was the nature of their decision-making at crucial points in their lives, and on what world view was it based?

The testimonies give fascinating glimpses into these areas of speculation. They may be read as the narrative of assembly service which guides the thinking and activities of those in full-time service. These men are the role models and opinion formers within the assemblies, so their narrative is of considerable importance for an understanding of the tight Brethren.

A Brethren Upbringing

All but 3 of the 58 accounts included descriptions of the writer's upbringing, specifying the presence or absence, and the nature, of their parents' religious observance. Nine parental couples were not churchgoers, 12 were attenders at other denominations, and 34, almost two-thirds, were in assembly fellowship.

Almost without exception, these latter parents are described as being completely 'faithful' Brethren; that is, they were dutiful attenders at all the assembly meetings and at local Brethren conferences. The extent to which this degree of religious observance dominated the socialization of their children cannot be exaggerated. The testimonies describe a continual round of domestic and assembly activities, for example:

> Farm work, or the many constraints of business life, all had to take a back seat to the priority of going to meeting....We attended all the conferences in our vicinity.

Continuous religious practice became normalized, to be accepted without question. Writing for *Precious Seed*,[1] a couple ask where they went wrong in 'training up their children in the way that they should go'. Within weeks of their birth, the children attended the Breaking of Bread and Sunday School and the first half of conferences. When they were old enough to keep awake, they attended the (Sunday evening) Gospel Service. As soon as they could read, they went to the children's Bible Study. And, of course, at home they participated in daily family Bible reading and prayer.

All went well until late teenage, when their personal Bible study petered out and they stopped attending meetings. They remain convinced of their salvation, and continue to have good relations with their parents. The parents' principal sadness, however, stems from their "lack of spiritual interest, and a lifestyle so different to what we taught them" (possibly code for leaving the assembly and rejecting its doctrine of separation from 'the world'). The parents live in hope, however, that "'ere long, they will return to the Lord and put Him at the centre of their lives".

Brethren parents placed the highest importance on the Christian upbringing of their children, and especially upon their *salvation*. Salvation is always construed as a single event in time, before which the child is unsaved and after which it is saved. It requires the instant transition from one spiritual state to its opposite. A letter to *Believer's Magazine's* regular feature, Question Box, asks: "Is it possible for one to be saved at such a young age that the date and time cannot be remembered?" The response comes clear and strong:

> It is a fact that not all genuine believers can recall the exact time when they were converted. However, such should be able to look back to an experience when, in all their need, they came to Christ for salvation. Salvation is not a process; it is an event, a definite experience. The individual is brought to a point of conviction of sin by the Holy Spirit. This is followed by 'repentance toward God, and faith toward our Lord Jesus Christ'. (Acts 20.21)

Extreme youth does not seem to be an obstacle. These testimonies indicate that many of those who were brought up in Brethren families were saved at an age somewhere between 6 and 11. This is hardly surprising, given that "both parents had a great desire that their children would come to know Christ as Saviour", or "my parents persuaded me from my earliest years of my guilt and need for the atoning sacrifice of Jesus Christ", or "our parents read and prayed with the family daily, and always had our salvation as the priority".

Now, of course, these preoccupations of their parents were expressed and construed in theological language such as 'conviction of sin', 'atonement', and 'repentance'. However, from a psychological perspective, profound feelings of guilt and fear are a frequent concomitant. Both of these emotions were elicited in the following—doubtless extreme—episode: an evangelist, FC, is staying with the writer's family while preaching a series of sermons. At the time the writer was aged six. He recounts:

FC asked me to retrieve for him from the porch a long rusty nail, which I did. Quietly and solemnly, he pressed that long nail into the palm of my hand until I thought surely he would break the skin. He explained the sufferings of the Lord Jesus upon Calvary to me and repeated often that the reason for those sufferings was because of who I was and what I had done. The seriousness of sin against God never left me and frequently arose in my thinking sometimes while in school and many times while alone in bed. I tried often to understand the preaching of the gospel, hoping to find relief from the consciousness of my sin before God.

Feeling personally guilty for the death of Christ was an extreme outcome, but a more general sense of guilt for sin and sins was common. The other emotion consequent upon Brethren gospel preaching was fear. A general fear of punishment was not too difficult to induce in a family environment in which it was common practice to physically punish ('chasten') for misdeeds.

But a more particular fear was caused by the eschatological doctrine of the Rapture. This Brethren theological preoccupation has profound psychological impact. For if you face young children with the possibility that their parents may be suddenly transported away from them into heaven, it is hardly surprising that they suffer acute separation anxiety.

"I knew if the Lord had to come," writes a once terrified Brother, "loved ones would be taken and I would be left for the judgment and wrath of God". Another writer remembers: "The coming of the Lord was the thing that troubled me most, and many a time I wakened up at night thinking that the great event had taken place and that I was left for the judgment of God".

And in a particularly distressing account, a boy arrives unexpectedly to find his father not at home:

"Sitting there alone that late summer evening, the thought suddenly occurred to me that the Lord had come and caught away the loved ones who were saved. I cannot express the pang of agony which I then experienced". The father returns home from business later, but the experience "left an impression upon my mind which did not readily pass away, and many a night afterwards I slipped out of bed, tip-toed to my parents' bedroom door, and peeped in to see if they were still there".

So it was hardly surprising that Brethren children wanted to be saved as desperately as their parents wanted them to be:

I cannot recall any occasion in my life when I didn't want to be saved. I respected those who were saved because I knew they will be among the citizens of heaven – I would have given anything to have what they had.

Given that getting saved was the recommended and approved means of reducing their burden of fear and guilt, it is hardly surprising that so many grasped this opportunity at so young an age. What is more surprising is that they often found it an immensely difficult task.

But what must be most surprising of all to those unfamiliar with fundamentalisms is that not a single one of these eminent and esteemed Brethren testifiers demonstrated the slightest qualm about this process. No moral issues regarding the relationship of means to ends appeared to have occurred to them, let alone any doubts regarding the nature and desirability of the end itself. On the contrary, they could not praise their parents and the visiting preachers highly enough for enabling their salvation. And there was no indication that they intended to act any differently in their own ministry or towards their own children.

In fact, they were acting in complete accordance with their dualist world view. They see themselves as living in the sixth and penultimate dispensation, the Church Age. In this present age, their self-concept is as spiritual rather than natural agents. All their decisions, including how they bring up their children, are based upon spiritual, heavenly, rather than carnal, worldly criteria. Their primary parental aim must therefore be the salvation and spiritual development of their children within the assembly. The idea of mental health or illness is a human, not a scriptural concept, and should be explained in terms of the activities of Satan and his devils.

Getting Saved

These Brethren children, then, were under a lot of pressure. Their parents made it clear that their priority was for the children to be saved, and the dutiful search to fulfil this expectation was likely to have been a source of anxiety and concern. Parents (and preachers) sought to help children get saved by inducing feelings of guilt about sin and fear of punishment and loss. But instead of relieving the guilt and fear, the process of getting saved can itself become a further problem. A Brethren childhood could be a worrying time indeed.

The power of anxiety to inhibit all response and render the individual frozen into inaction is a clinical cliché. Time after time, the testimonies report opportunities to get saved being missed, much to the child's disappointment. The usual adult salvation narrative has the convert being tugged away by the attraction of sin and the power of the Satan. Brethren children, on the contrary, desperately want to get saved, but find it a terrible struggle.

The writers' accounts speak for themselves:

> On the 29th of July, shortly before going out to the meeting, I was in my room with my Bible seeking, as I had often sought, for a verse to give peace to my soul...At that moment I remembered that I had heard so many tell of being saved through these verses and I was understanding nothing. This came as a shock to me, as I realised that there was no salvation for me, and that I had already sealed my choice for hell and the lake of fire for ever. I, trembling, went to the meeting and listened almost having lost hope of ever being saved.

Again:

> I tried to believe, and waited but nothing happened....I stayed in the kitchen determined that I would not go to bed until my sins were forgiven. I sat there reading again and again the well-known verses but I seemed to be in total darkness. At last, exhausted and weary, the thought came to my mind 'you will never be saved', and I trembled at this thought as I saw before me only the flames of hell for ever and ever.

And finally:

> I was deeply concerned about my soul, and wanted to be saved. Being brought up as I was, however, I thought that I knew how to be saved........ The meetings closed, and I was still in my sins.......Salvation now became my chief concern. I read different gospel booklets and asked God to save me, but no light came..........On the Tuesday night of that fourth week of meetings, my closest brother John came home saying that he had been saved during the meeting. He told me that it was very easy, which annoyed me, as we had before agreed that it was very difficult.

Indeed, so anxious were children to comply with parental hopes that some made a so-called false profession. This involved saying that you had been saved when you did not think you really had been. To quote:

I was naturally shy, and it embarrassed me when people asked me if I was saved. I suppose because of this, I told people who asked me that I was saved, even though I knew I wasn't. Some would ask me when and how. I know they meant well, but because of my shyness I made up a story telling people a time, place, and manner how God saved me. It was not a false profession in the normal sense of the word. I knew it was false and the longing to be saved never left me.

Another boy, having experienced the recommended sequence of events to secure his salvation, even started 'fearing a false profession' immediately afterwards.

The relief from fear and guilt consequent upon getting saved is palpable. These emotions had not only been developed over the entire period of the child's socialization, but also stimulated by repeated attendance at series of gospel meetings addressed daily by a visiting evangelist. Furthermore, particular events had frequently raised the emotional temperature even further, for example: the death of a parent, grandparent, or friend; being picked out by name in public as still being unsaved; siblings being saved before them; or the experience of a near fatal accident. Hence the following reactions to successfully getting saved are unsurprising:

> At that moment I realised that the finished work of Christ on the cross had satisfied the demands of a sin-hating God and was enough to meet my great need, and I simply trusted Him as my Saviour. What a relief to know that my sins were all forgiven and that I would never find myself in hell.

Again:

> On returning home, I ran ahead to tell my mother when she came to the door. There was great rejoicing in our home and my own heart was full to overflowing.

And finally:

> In a very real and personal way at that moment I grasped the great Gospel truth 'Christ died for me'. The burden went and joy entered my soul and I simply said 'I believe I'm now saved' and there was rejoicing and thanksgiving as we all went back to bed.

Of course, all these testimonies are from those who succeeded in getting saved. We do not hear of the outcomes for those who failed.

THE CALL TO SERVICE

The next major signpost along the formation of the tight Brethren elite is the experience of vocation. Just as the young Brethren child is prepared for salvation, so too they are made ready to respond to the call of the Holy Spirit to full-time work for the Lord, either in their home country or abroad.

The first major step towards this final destination is prepared in childhood, as stories of missionary exploits are told at home and in Sunday School, and visiting evangelists and missionaries stay in the family home while they conduct local campaigns or give reports on their work.

After conversion, baptism, and reception into assembly fellowship, the next step is a set of developmental tasks aimed at testing and training for future service. These include teaching Sunday School, youth work, tract distribution, open-air meetings, and hospital and door-to-door visiting. On many of these activities, the young believer will be accompanied by an experienced brother, who can act as a role model and also assess the tyro's suitability for bigger things.

If he shows promise, he will be invited by a full-time evangelist to accompany the latter on a series of meetings and play a part in the local campaign. He acts in an apprentice role to a master preacher or pair of preachers. Such apprentices are often highly impressed and deeply influenced by these mentors:

> These men were down to earth, far from preacherfied professionals. They had a vision for souls and for the needs of the work. I thank God for them, some of whom have early left us. They taught us to pray, to preach, how to deal with difficult people and questions at the door. They were our mentors and our role models. They took us under their wing and made us part of their lives.

Next typically arrives the period of 'exercise', that is, being prompted to come to a decision regarding the surrender of paid secular employment and the dedication to full-time work for the Lord. Many experience a specific call, and several explicitly liken this to their conversion.

It can be immediate, powerful, and emotionally overwhelming:

> I can remember a time of deep soul searching and waiting on God. For about a week I had no desire for food. One day on my knees, with my Bible open before me, I was reading from Romans chapter one...It was while meditating on these portions that the Lord spoke to me in a real way. I

totally surrendered my will to His Will. I knew that He had a purpose for my life, and that I was willing to follow wherever He would lead. The burden was lifted. The tears flowed. My appetite for food returned. To me, this memory is just as real as the night that He reached out and saved me.

And again:

> I was very low as to this very important step that was burdening me, and was God calling me. I had time to think and pray, the burden to serve God was so heavy I wanted to get rid of it, so in frustration one afternoon I said to the Lord 'If this burden is Thine, keep it there, if not please remove it'. The burden did not go, so I had peace that I should step out for God.

It was hardly surprising that the writers found their situation a burden. The pressures put on them were nearly as great as those put on Brethren children to get saved. Full-time evangelists and missionaries, or just local overseers, were not slow to urge them to obey the call. "When are you going to stop wasting your time lecturing and get on with the Lord's work", said one.

Or, to take another example, a

> Welsh brother who was working in the Rhone valley among Moslems [sic].....started asking me if I had any interest in giving myself to the Lord. I admitted that I did have in the past, but did not divulge my more recent thoughts. He started to speak to me very directly and pointed out the need to be exercised definitely before the Lord. He really stirred me up....

By way of a gentle hint, a brother was sent a textbook of introductory Spanish. Or, most peremptory of all, another received a letter from a senior brother consisting of one word only: 'Tanzania'!

Being adults by now, the writers hesitated before taking the huge step of giving up a regular income. Their choice was either to survive in their home country 'living by faith', that is, dependent on donations mainly from their commending (sponsoring) assemblies, or to transport their dependents overseas similarly without visible means of support. To help them take their decision in line with God's will, they looked for signs, that is, divine indications that they should or should not go. In other words, they expected a supernatural intervention which would constitute a clear signal one way or the other.

The most frequent event which the writers chose to treat as divine guidance was the sudden appearance in their minds of a specific biblical text, which was interpretable in terms of their situation. Other such meaningful events indicating divine approval or disapproval were the granting or refusal of a visa, the saving of souls in their present evangelistic activities, and the successful sale of their business or house.

So eager were some of the writers to gain certainty of the correctness of their decision that they set terms for the Almighty in which to communicate His advice:

> Whether right or wrong, we asked the Lord to graciously answer our prayer by giving to us three evidences of water upon the fleece [this refers to an Old Testament story in the book of Judges chapter 6, in which Jehovah confirmed Gideon's leadership by a sign]. Firstly, that our overseers would approach us on their own and ask us if we were thinking in this way. Secondly, that one of the Lord's servants would write to us and ask if we were exercised about the work. Thirdly, that the Lord would in due order bring a buyer for our house that it would be evident that it was Himself that sent them.

All these signs came to pass, and so divine approval was inferred and a full-time career 'in the work' was begun.

While anguishing over the spiritual reality of the call occupied a lot of their time, however, the same attention was not always paid to the practical details of training and preparation for the task ahead. To quote:

> We arrived in Brazil on the 5th of November 1947, with a two-year-old son Stanley, little money in our pockets, knowing nobody in the land, and not speaking the Portuguese language.

So Heavenly Minded

These accounts of the writers' call reveal the same fundamental dualism of the tight Brethren world view as was evident in their accounts of their salvation. The most fundamental binary distinction is between God and Man, the spiritual and the carnal, the godly and the worldly, the supernatural and the natural. Each of these binaries has somewhat different connotations, but all share the same evaluative contrast: the good versus the bad.

The logical implications of this duality for the process of the vocational call are obvious. The decision which they take has to be God's decision rather than their own. The decision itself, the signals by which it is indicated, and the actions which ensue, all have to be convincingly attributed to the Almighty.

This is where the supernatural versus natural binary becomes important. The writers typically request a sign or signs from God as to whether they really are called to serve full-time. An event is often attributed to God's agency if it is unexpected or difficult to explain. For example, a biblical verse has to suddenly present itself to the writer's mind; a brother who barely knows him mentions to him the very course of action he is already contemplating; a loved one who has long remained unsaved is wonderfully converted; a visa which has been repeatedly denied is after all granted. In sum, these events are understood as unexpected, inexplicable, and hence supernatural, the work of the Holy Spirit.

The contrast, of course, is with Man's work (rather than God's), which requires rationality, organization, and preparation (rather than faith and trust). The former usually results in missionaries receiving training in the language and culture of the country where they are to serve and a program of induction upon arrival. The consequences of the latter are their sudden arrival penniless, ignorant of local culture and language, and without a plan of action. This is the same logic my father was rejecting when he made notes in his Bible rather than giving utterance "as the Spirit led". According to the Brethren belief system, the value and practice of analysis and reason are 'human', 'of Man', and therefore evil.

The same fundamental dichotomy is evident in the act of leaving one's secular employment for the full-time work for the Lord. For several of the writers, the increasing demands on their time and energy made by the assemblies were causing them problems in fulfilling their obligations to their employer. Whom should they consider their master—Man or God? Should they remain 'of the world', or should they 'serve the Lord'?

There is only one answer open to a devout Brother when the question is framed like this. Both the question and the answer clearly follow from the binary world view. This is the world view which enables an esteemed Brother to advise, "You're wasting your time lecturing". It results in writers from a wide range of occupations—among them, lumberjack, engineer, teacher, technician, farmer, lorry driver, air traffic controller, policeman, builder, and shopkeeper—treating their work as merely a means of earning a living. Ultimately, it results in a doctor serving overseas as a missionary with his wife, a nurse, asserting that his sole aim is to save souls. It causes a builder to ruminate, "Here I am building houses, and at the same time thousands [are] dying in their sins". Both are so constrained by the stark binary contrasts of their belief system that they cannot entertain the possibility that saving lives or building houses can be the work of God to which they are called. That spiritual experience is reserved for saving souls and building up the saints: 'the Lord's work'.

These reflections upon the episode of call lead conveniently on to the following chapters. For the 'Assembly Truth' that justifies the whole process of conversion, formation, and call is derived from the attribution of *authority* to God's Word, the Bible, and its interpretation by the Brethren. And the critique of the world and the natural Man point to the supreme value placed upon the believer's *separation* from others. Authority and separation are the two key Brethren themes, and their prominence in the Brethren social identity provides Brothers and Sisters with confidence, certainty, and self-esteem. They also firm up the fundamentalist separation from, and denigration of, the other global social systems than religion. Separation from other religions and other Christians completes the impregnability of these boundaries against everyone else.

Summary

The written testimonies of Brethren who are full-time preachers or missionaries overseas reveal a similar emphasis to the obituaries on spiritual experience. The two key events in these narratives are conversion and call. By far the majority of these esteemed Brethren were brought up in Brethren families or, in some cases, in families fully practising in other denominations or sects. Nevertheless, a conversion experience was mandatory, and was the dominant aim of Brethren parents for their children. For many children, its achievement was difficult and anxious. The later vocational call to full-time work for the Lord was a similarly emotive and problematic event. It had to be seen to come from God, so its discernment was difficult. Events had to be interpreted as messages from the Almighty, despite the obvious availability of other explanations for their occurrence. The testimonies point up the binary opposites which define the Brethren world view: spiritual versus worldly, God versus Man, faith versus reason, and so on.

NOTE

1. Train up a child in the way he should go, Precious Seed, 2011, vol. 67, no. 2, (anonymous).

Authority

CHAPTER 8

Conformity and Belief

THE INDIVIDUAL AND THE COLLECTIVE

From this point on, I will concentrate on the tight Brethren faction only. This is partly because the loose Brethren are varied in their beliefs and practices, whereas the tight ones are much more homogeneous, so generalizations can more confidently be made about them. But more important, the tight Brethren appear to exhibit the characteristic features of fundamentalism.[1] These are, first, their preoccupation with authority, as exercised in their case by the Bible (Part II); and second, their hostility to modernity, expressed in terms of their separation from it in all its shapes and forms (Part III). The aims of this book are to try to understand the Brethren not only as a sect but also as an archetypical example of fundamentalism. I then conclude in Part IV by trying to explore the relationship of fundamentalism to modern religion in a globalizing world.[2,3,4]

So, why is the issue of *authority* so important for the Brethren? What is the basis for authority in the assemblies, and how is it maintained and exercised? How can we understand it from a social scientific point of view? Before we start, the key argument in Chap. 5 bears recapitulation: any worthwhile social psychological account emphasizes that social influence is a two-way process. Yes, there are many ways in which other people influence individual Brothers and Sisters. Parents, assemblies, elders, preachers, and writers all help to instil the tight Brethren culture—its beliefs, values, norms, and practices. But on the other hand, individual

© The Author(s) 2018

P. Herriot, *The Open Brethren: A Christian Sect in the Modern World*,
https://doi.org/10.1007/978-3-030-03219-7_8

adherents alone or together can sometimes cause change in the culture, acting upon it rather than being acted upon.[5]

The picture of the tight Brethren which emerged from the first six chapters was, nevertheless, one of a social system characterized by internal integration and homogeneity, with a high degree of conformity to its culture. Power is exercised to ensure conformity and prevent change. Beliefs, values, norms, and practices are held sacrosanct, and non-conformists are made to feel unwelcome and 'unsound'.

Similar effort is put into maintaining boundaries between assemblies and other social systems, both religious and secular. Again, control by others to ensure separation is exercised in terms of disapproval of any sort of contact other than for purposes of evangelism, paying taxes, or earning a living. Individuals who refuse to conform to this culture often find themselves in the position of the loose Brethren. Unwilling to isolate themselves to this degree, they are frequently the object of outright public denunciation as unsound and apostate. Thus one of the twin themes emphasized in my father's notes—authority—is in prominent view.

There is, however, a sense in which, even within the tight Brethren, individuals can be self-directed and behave as such rather than as other-directed: as active subjects rather than as passive objects. Certainly, particularly in the case of those born into a Brethren family, there is strong social pressure to conform to the culture and internalize it as part of one's self, one's social identity. But what is internalized can generate its own outcomes in terms of individual actions. While tight Brethren may look for behavioural conformity as well as orthodoxy of belief, it is impossible to legislate for every activity in a complex late-modern society. There is room for adherents to formulate their own intentions and actions (but only, and it is a big 'but', if they are in accord with the foundational beliefs of the culture).

THE CONFORMITY PROCESS

We often use the idea of conformity to refer to overt behaviour only, as distinct from internal beliefs and values—'*mere* conformity'. A favourite national story has British prisoners of war in World War II cheerfully obeying the orders of their captors while secretly burrowing their way out of the prison camp to rejoin the fight for freedom.

The socialization of Brethren children is not solely concerned with the transmission of rules about how to behave, however. Rather, from the very beginning, it seeks to transmit the sect's culture *as a whole*: its beliefs and values as well as its norms and practices.[6] Chapter 7 suggested the profound effects this can have on children. Children generally need to gain the approval of their parents and acquire confidence in their attachment to them. Many childhood anxieties relate to the loss of parental affection and to the possibility of separation. Add to this the tenuous boundaries between childhood imagination and reality and the blurred distinction between literal and figurative meanings, and the writers' personal tales of childhood terror and paralysis of action in the previous chapter are perfectly understandable.

The case of (many) Brethren children is best understood in terms of one of the classic forms of social pressure—the exploitation of dependence, in particular of the need to belong and gain others' approval (affiliation). The case of the older converts, however, is rather different. The converts may be from another Christian denomination, or they may be hitherto entirely unchurched. In the former case, the converts from the 'sects' will know little of the unusual ecclesiastical practices of the Brethren, and probably will have a less separatist world view. In search of certainty, they will be open to detailed instruction regarding 'Assembly Truth' authoritatively presented. The unchurched, on the other hand, will have little clue as to what to believe and value and how to act, let alone about what to do in assembly meetings. In both cases they want clarity.[7]

This is not to say, of course, that adult converts are only driven by needs of meaning and certainty. Like Brethren children, they too will be motivated by the need for affiliation and belonging,[8] or for relief from fear and worry. Indeed, research indicates that many adult converts to Christianity are, at the time of their conversion, experiencing crises in their lives of one sort or another.[9]

How then is this normative social influence exercised? How does it work? I argued in Chap. 5 that the Brethren are characterized by extreme differentiation from other social systems, but also by extreme integration within each assembly and to a considerable degree, with other 'like-minded' assemblies. Internal homogeneity presents the individual with a clear model of the approved culture, for there is little variability among the Brothers and Sisters, and therefore little ambiguity. Moreover, the social pressure to conform will be exercised on the same issues, since these are universally agreed to be the ones which matter. Strongly held beliefs and values regarding gender roles, for example, result in issues regarding female dress and deportment becoming extremely important.

The social influence of the majority is both directed and enforced by the only universally appointed authority figures: the overseers, or elders. They exercise pastoral and doctrinal control (over behaviour and belief). In line with the belief system which tends to attribute actions to God or Satan, overseers are appointed by the Holy Spirit (not by themselves or existing overseers). This divine authority is actualized as the judgement of the existing overseers that a brother has the spiritual gifts required for the role.

Thus the only visible form of leadership is self-perpetuating in nature. There is no fixed term of office—the obituaries reviewed in Chap. 6 sometimes refer to 30 and 40 years continuously in post. With such absence of turnover and obscurity of process, it is hardly surprising that the leadership emphasizes conformity to existing culture rather than its adaptation to the changing social environment. Or, metaphorically speaking, that it insists on building up the ramparts rather than permitting the drawbridge to be lowered to allow passage into and out from the spiritual castle.

Leaders and followers, then, are united in exercising social control via conformity to the culture. Leaders are prototypes of the adherents—they represent ideal models of the stereotype of the good Brother.[10] The only real opportunity for change comes from input from visiting full-time preachers who circulate among groups of assemblies. Even in this case, however, doctrine is protected, since visiting preachers are invited by the 'communicating brother', usually one of the overseers, who chooses to invite only those known to be 'sound in Assembly Truth'.

The only other potential initiators of change are younger Brothers and Sisters whose experience outside the assembly has broadened their horizons. However, it is a well-established finding that leaders of change are more likely to be accepted and followed if they are perceived as 'one of us'.[11] In psychological terms, followers need to see leaders putting their own selves, their own social identities, on the line as well as those of their followers. It is hardly surprising that many younger Brothers and Sisters despair of the possibility of change and adaptation and leave for other churches. The only change they can see happening is different issues taking salient position as new threats are perceived from 'the world'. Decades ago it was the cinema; now it's social media.

But how are tight Brethren successful in ensuring conformity to the culture? Where does their authority come from? It can, they believe, only come from one source: God Himself. And God's will is spoken clearly and directly to believers through His Word, the Bible.

BIBLICAL TRUTH

If the Brethren culture is constituted by beliefs, values, and norms of behaviour, what is the relation between these elements? How, in other words, do adherents come to formulate their intentions to act in certain ways rather than others? Well-established theoretical models of decision-making[12] suggest that intentions to act are a product of beliefs and values, moderated by social norms. We may *believe* that preaching the gospel every Sunday evening at 6.30 pm is an appropriate mode of evangelism, and we may place a high *value* on saving souls. Further, this method is the regular and *approved* assembly practice. Hence, we have every *intention* to continue holding the gospel service for the foreseeable future. However, repeated experience demonstrates that no unsaved sinners attend the gospel service, and therefore souls cannot be saved.

From a pragmatic perspective, this experience should lead to a change of belief. We can no longer rationally believe that the gospel service is an effective (and therefore appropriate) mode of evangelism if no 'unsaved' even attend. But this is typically not what happens. The gospel service continues to be conducted, and the lack of converts is attributed to the wiles of the Satan.

The explanation for this apparently irrational behaviour is the dominance of *a single 'root' belief* from which all other Brethren beliefs and values, and therefore all practices and behaviour, are derived. This belief is that the Bible is the Word of God directly speaking to each of His people, giving them clear instruction as to what they should believe, what they should value, and how they should act.

Scriptural guidance is *inerrant*, regarding matters historical, scientific, ethical, and all else. It is *timeless*, applicable to modern as much as to ancient biblical times. It is *universal*, not relative to particular cultures or situations. It is *unequivocal*, since there can be no doubt about its meaning, and it certainly does not contradict itself. Would the Almighty have expressed His will in obscure ways, to make it hard for us? No, the meaning is plain to see, and the sense is the obvious and apparent one. In the case of the example of the gospel service, the Bible clearly tells us that we are to preach the gospel, so we carry on faithfully doing so.

It is worth re-emphasizing that the root belief is that the Bible contains everything we need to know. Appeal to any other source is not permitted. If there is some doubt about whether a passage is to be read as (literal) history or as (metaphorical) poetry, the Bible itself will indicate which genre is being used. Whatever the genre, however, the truth which is revealed is absolute. We may note at this point Ralph Hood's wry comment: "nothing is more variable than the perception of absolute truth".[13] The 'plain reading' of the text may present different 'plain meanings' to different readers, particularly when it is full of symbolic references, as in the books of Daniel and Revelation.

Given this root belief, the decision to continue holding the gospel service is perfectly logical. More importantly, an entire and broad ranging belief system follows, provided that the basic assumption is accepted. If we believe that a set of documents written in premodern times provides us with absolute, universal, and unequivocal truth, then we will be forced to accept a pre-modern view of the late-modern world.

One consequence of holding the root belief is a particular view of *the nature of reality itself.* Just as the Bible is God's direct Word to humankind, unaffected by the human writers of its different books, so reality in general is determined by God's will, not by human agency. Various unusual or unexpected or important events are specifically noted as being attributable to God's direct agency, and described in supernatural terms. Obvious examples are the biblical accounts of the creation of the world, various miraculous appearances or healings, and the second coming of Christ. God does, however, permit sinful humankind to engage in acts of folly, using these as signs that His second coming and final judgement are going to happen soon.

Other premodern historical, social, political, and religious perspectives typical of the era of the biblical writers are taken for granted as the divine order of things. *History* is described in terms of the sequence of God's dealings with humankind and in particular with His chosen people. 'History is His story', as the preachers of my childhood put it. Past, present, and future are all divinely determined, and in the latter's case, predictable. *Socially,* patriarchy was the order of the day, with slaves and women all subordinates in the household. *Politically,* power was held by emperor and/or clan. In *religious* terms, God was perceived as the God of Israel, or in the New Testament, He was the source of spiritual salvation and inspiration for the local assemblies.

Any religious movement or sect which treats the Bible as the inerrant and universal Word of God is going to accept as absolute truth these premodern assumptions about reality, history, society, politics, and religion which permeate its pages.

However, it is impossible to detach beliefs and doctrines from the overall culture of a social system. Beliefs and values predict intentions and actions at an individual and a group level. Consequently, Brethren frequently find themselves acting in counter-cultural ways: and actions are generally more visible than ideas. The remaining chapters of Part II explore these connexions in depth. However, here we may note briefly some examples of beliefs and their implications from previous chapters:

- Believers cannot affect the course of history, since its course is already determined by God; they should therefore not engage in social or political action.
- Humankind is by nature born sinful; therefore every effort should be made to get people saved, from their earliest childhood onward.
- Decisions should be taken on the basis of divine guidance, revealed supernaturally.
- Christ is returning to rapture believers soon, a fact which we should use to help sinners get saved.
- The true church (i.e. the assemblies) are God's special people, the new Israel; our duty of love and care is primarily to our own people.
- St Paul urged the Ephesians that wives should submit to their husbands; this should be a central principle of family and church life. And so on.

THEORETICAL SUMMARY

The overall theoretical perspective of the second part of the book, then, is aimed at understanding the role played by authority for the tight Brethren. It incorporates two different traditions of social psychological explanation.

The first of these seeks to explain the effect of the collective on the individual. Its main idea is that of *conformity*. Social influence is identified as the main process by which the culture of any social system – its beliefs, values, and norms of behaviour – are communicated to individuals so that they accept them and internalise them as part of who they think they are.

People may conform for a variety of reasons. They may be unsure what to think or how to act, and welcome the certainty which the culture offers. They may experience pressure from a majority in their social environment, and therefore conform in order to gain and retain their acceptance and approval. They may join up because being part of the social system in question makes them feel good about themselves; it enhances their self-esteem or their social status. They may feel under the control of high status authority figures who require obedience (although in this case the conformity may only be in terms of compliant behaviour rather than of beliefs and values).

Non-conformity (and therefore the possibility of change in the culture) is likewise explained in this tradition in terms of social process. Minority influence is often difficult to exert, but can be effective when individuals or minorities focus on specific beliefs or values or more often, actions.[14] Minority influence, in other words, is often content based, whereas majority influence frequently relies on leaders' status or established rules and precedents. A minority can persuade an assembly to join in a local evangelistic mission, for example, or to permit the gospel hall to be used for a children's nursery.

A second theoretical tradition, however, is more focussed on the *content* of the culture as a determinant of group and individual behaviour. Rather than seeking to understand how social influence is established and exerted, it addresses the question of how the culture of a social system is expressed in action.

In particular, this tradition examines the structure and content of *belief systems* and their relationships with each other. These relationships may involve the relative importance of particular beliefs within the overall belief system. The theory then explores how such systems, which include beliefs about value priorities as well as about the nature of reality, lead groups and individuals to act in particular ways.

The two theoretical traditions therefore take different perspectives. The first is concerned with social influence being exerted upon individuals and groups to conform to a culture. The second emphasises the internalised culture as a determinant of actions, which are usually conformist but may be non-conformist. Any useful discussion of authority in the tight Brethren, I argue, needs to take account of both of these traditions if it is to offer a rounded understanding. It has to explain not only how the assembly culture becomes influential and internalised, but also how its particular beliefs lead to a typical Brethren life.

Summary

The Brethren culture—its beliefs, values, and rules of behaviour—is all instilled from childhood. The most important element is belief. The root belief is that the Bible is the Word of God transmitted directly to the believer, and that it tells you all you need to know about doctrine and practice. Since the Bible expresses the worldview and culture of premodern societies, modern believers are being asked to conform to a radically different counter-culture. The teaching and approval (or disapproval) of family and assembly generally exercise sufficient social influence to ensure conformity. The young are left in little doubt as to what is expected of them, since there is hardly any variation in the prototype of a model Brother and Sister. However, the Bible, although it is very detailed in its prescriptions in some aspects of behaviour, cannot possibly spell out all the behavioural rules for a complex modern society. Potential for the stimulation of change in assembly culture by individuals or minorities lies in this ambiguity about action.

NOTES

1. Almond, Gabriel, Appleby, R. Scott, & Sivan, Emmanuel (2003) Strong Religion: The Rise of Fundamentalisms around the World. Chicago: University of Chicago Press.
2. Robertson, Roland (1992) Globalization: Social Theory and Global Culture. London: Sage.
3. Beyer, Peter (2006) Religions in Global Society. London: Routledge.
4. Casanova, Jose (1994) Public Religions in the Modern World. Chicago: University of Chicago Press.
5. Martin, Robin, & Hewstone, Miles (2003) Social-influence processes of control and change: Conformity, obedience to authority, and innovation. In Michael Hogg & Joel Cooper (eds) Handbook of Social Psychology. London: Sage.
6. Schein, Edward (1985) Organizational Culture and Leadership. San Francisco: Jossey-Bass.
7. Hogg, Michael & Mullin, Barbara-Anne (1999) Joining groups to reduce uncertainty. In Dominic Abrams & Michael Hogg (eds) Social Identity and Social Cognition. Oxford: Blackwell.
8. Hine, Robert (1997) Relationships: A Dialectical Perspective. Hove: Psychology Press.
9. Spilka, Bernard, Hood, Ralph, Hunsberger, Bruce, & Gorsuch, Richard (2003) The Psychology of Religion (3rd edn) ch 11. New York: Guilford.
10. Hogg, Michael & Abrams, Dominic (2003) Intergroup behaviour and social identity. In Michael Hogg & Joel Cooper (eds) Handbook of Social Psychology. London: Sage.

11. Hogg, Michael (2001) Social identification, group prototypicality, and emergent leadership. In Michael Hogg & Deborah Terry (eds) Social Identity Processes in Organizational Contexts. Philadelphia PA: Psychology Press.
12. Fishbein, Martin & Ajzen, Izcek (1975) Belief, Attitude, Intention, and Behaviour. London: Addison-Wesley.
13. Hood, Ralph, Hill, Peter, & Williamson, Paul (2005) The Psychology of Religious Fundamentalism, p. 27. New York: Guilford.
14. Moscovici, Serge (1985) Social influence and conformity. In Gardner Lindsay & Elliot Aronson (eds) The Handbook of Social Psychology (3rd edn) vol. 2. New York: Random House.

CHAPTER 9

Authority in Action

Assembly Truth

So much for the theory. But how does authority look in practice? One fruitful source of evidence is the Question and Answer feature in two of the tight Brethren magazines, the *Believer's Magazine* (2005–2017) and *Precious Seed* (2009–2017). Once again, then, the most recent numbers of these journals have been chosen for analysis, in order to demonstrate that we are considering current, not historical, tight Brethren culture.

It is not just the *answers* which reflect authoritarian beliefs and attitudes, but also the *questions*. These magazines do not reveal authority figures seeking to impose strict doctrine and conduct on recalcitrant or lukewarm followers. Rather, the questioners are positively begging to be given precise instructions about what to believe and how to behave. This shows that the sect itself is demonstrably authoritarian throughout, leaders and at least some followers alike.

The questions submitted by readers are concerned with a relatively restricted range of topics: discipline and practice in the assembly; the differing roles of Brothers and Sisters; the correct interpretation of biblical passages; and finally, believers' separation from the world. They are, in other words, related to Assembly Truth. I will deal with the first of these topics, assembly discipline, here, and the others in later chapters.

It is hardly surprising that 'Assembly Truth' is a central theme, for the claim that they are the only true New Testament church is what differentiates the tight Brethren from others. To ensure conformity to this belief

© The Author(s) 2018   83
P. Herriot, *The Open Brethren: A Christian Sect in the Modern World*,
https://doi.org/10.1007/978-3-030-03219-7_9

and practice is therefore a primary concern, since the continued existence of any sect depends on maintaining its differentiator. And that difference will not be clearly evident unless all adherents proclaim it unanimously and unambiguously both in word and deed. There can be no wooliness at the boundaries, since this will blur the difference between the assemblies and the rest.

The primacy of 'Assembly Truth' is reflected in a reader's question: "Is the way we gather the most important issue in our Christian life?" The editorial respondent claims to be in a no-win situation. Some will say that Assembly Truth does indeed occupy this elevated position, he writes, but others will argue that this ignores the Scriptures regarding "how we should live day by day". That these appear as the only two alternatives speaks volumes of the importance he attaches to the former.

He then continues with a rose-tinted account of the foundation of the early church, when "in any one locality, all the believers would be united in their doctrines and practices". However, "error began to infiltrate, and eventually Christians fragmented into different groups". Readers are urged to "have a conviction about where and how we gather", and are reminded that "one of the principal objectives of this magazine is to help promote an adherence to scriptural doctrines concerning church practice". They are also reminded, however, that this conformity should be the product of their love for the Lord.

Questioners are extremely keen to discover what the rules of best assembly practice are. "Would it be in order to have a hymn or reading between breaking bread and drinking the cup?" they ask. Or "What might be the line drawn on musical accompaniment in praise and worship?" Or "The current trend is to 'dress down' for a gospel meeting. I understand that expensive clothing is not becoming to the gospel, but how far do we go in 'dressing down'?"

Respondents always make a distinction in replying to this type of question between what is optional and what is authoritative. What is optional is what is not explicitly required or forbidden by Scripture, and therefore is a matter of preference. The respondent does usually offer their own preference and their reasons for it. But what is authoritative is absolutely non-negotiable. Even if it puts people off and they leave, "we cannot subjugate biblical principles simply to maintain numbers; God's work must be done in God's way!" Sadly, however, some assemblies have undermined or deliberately set aside biblical principles, such as the silence of women in church, and faithful believers have felt unable to remain.

The questioners are thus being urged to ensure conformity to certain supposedly clear instructions in the New Testament as to assembly practice. So keen are they to do so that one writes back asking whether it is appropriate to invite a visiting preacher from a heretical assembly, even though the preacher himself is 'sound' regarding Assembly Truth.

CRIME AND PUNISHMENT

In all social systems, such zeal is normally accompanied by the desire for sanctions for non-conformity, and the Brethren are no exception. "Is ill health an evidence of God's chastening [punishment]?" asks a questioner innocently. Not usually, replies the respondent, but it is occasionally possible. After all, Ananias and Sapphira died as a result of "tempting the Spirit of the Lord" over a financial matter (Acts 5.9). And the behaviour of the Corinthian believers at the Breaking of Bread was so bad that "many were weak and sickly and many sleep" (1 Cor 11.29-30).

Death seems an extreme punishment, so the preferred sanction is excommunication. A seriously misbehaving Corinthian should be delivered "unto Satan for the destruction of the flesh, that the spirit may be saved in the day of the Lord Jesus, 1 Cor 5.4-5". Exploring the range of sanctions further, another questioner asks: "What is involved in withdrawing from a brother who walks disorderly? Is it the 'putting away' of 1 Corinthians 5, and what constitutes 'walking disorderly' (2 Thess 3.6)?" In the case of the Corinthians, the sin was immorality, the respondent answers [in Brethren terminology, 'immorality' refers to sexual misbehaviour]. This merits excommunication, whereas 'walking disorderly' refers to being idle, meddlesome, interfering, and needy. 'Withdrawing' from such persons simply means not getting mixed up or intimate with them, the cold shoulder treatment.

'Immorality' and 'walking disorderly' are mentioned by St Paul as justifying punishment in the assembly. But surely, suggests another questioner, there are many other violations of good assembly practice: "How long can saints in an assembly be allowed to absent themselves from some of the gatherings with no good cause, and what action should be taken?" he asks. "There is a sense", comes back the reply, "in which an individual puts himself out of fellowship by prolonged absence from the assembly with no good cause."

But what happens if the disobedient brother or sister repents? There must be limits to their readmission, exclaims a questioner:

Why was David not stoned for his adultery with Bathsheba? Would this mean that in this day of grace and (when there is the privilege of) assembly fellowship, he (David) would be able to fit into the assembly and exercise any gift that the Lord had given him? If, for example, he desired the office of an elder (1 Tim 3.1) in the Lord's assembly, would he be accepted?

The response may well have gratified the questioner: "such is the serious-ness of the sins committed that, if restored, he would never be free to exercise a public gift, and certainly never be recognised as an overseer".

A regimen of punishment has to be balanced with the prospect of reward, but administered proportionately to desserts. The questioner who asked "Will there be different levels of reward for believers?" is assured that at the final judgment seat of Christ, each individual will be rewarded according to the quantity and quality of their service to the Lord.

However, to qualify for service, believers have to meet various require-ments. They should, if not able to give the time and place of their conver-sion, at least be able to look back at a specific experience. Past sins do not necessarily prevent current service for the Lord, "but if we desire to be suitable for His service we need to ensure we are living sanctified lives".

Ensuring Conformity

Conformity is enforced in several ways. The approval or disapproval of the majority is a powerful instrument, but church order as required in Scripture decrees that authority should be vested in the oversight, the group of overseers or elders.

"How does the assembly recognize an elder," asks a questioner, "and what action should be taken when one who is recognized as an elder clearly does not fulfil his responsibilities?" The answer comes loud and clear: "It is the Holy Spirit who appoints elders or overseers through the Word of God". It is not the task of any outside body, and it certainly is not the right of the assembly itself to appoint its overseers—"the assembly is not a democratic institution".

How then is the divine mind to be discovered? The present overseers should take the lead when they see a brother showing the attributes required. These are specified in 1 Timothy 3.2: blameless, monoga-mous, vigilant, sober, well-behaved, hospitable, a good teacher, non-violent, not greedy, patient, not a brawler, not covetous, a good parent whose children are subject to him, not a novice, and of good report. The oversight should suggest to him that he should undertake the work of overseer, and express confidence in his ability to do so. He may, of course, himself have been 'exercised' by the Holy Spirit to volunteer.

From an external perspective, new overseers are appointed by a combination of the existing overseers and themselves. From a Brethren perspective, of course, this cannot be possible, since everything in the assembly is the work of the Holy Spirit, not of Man. The absence of any formal procedure or transparency in the process suggests the possibility of rule by the few, but the authoritarian attitudes of the assembly may well welcome this situation. However, in response to the final part of the question, the respondent writes that if an overseer ceases to manifest the qualities of an overseer, "the believers will cease to recognise him as an elder though he be one in name".

Assembly as Family

We know that fundamentalist believers are likely to be more authoritarian than average (see p. 42). If this is so, then we might expect to see this trait demonstrated in other areas of their life than the assembly. We should stress that it is just as likely they have developed more authoritarian attitudes as a consequence of their adherence as that they chose assembly fellowship as a consequence of existing attitudes.

One such area is *parenting*, and we have evidence that a Brethren upbringing typically emphasized obedience and conformity. In Chap. 7, it became evident that parents had very clear expectations about what their children should believe from a very early age. The story (see pp. 60–61) of the parents whose adult children now demonstrate "a lack of spiritual interest and a lifestyle so different to what we taught them"[1] is a painful example. Having imposed a demanding regime of home and assembly religious practice, they are at a loss as to why their children should leave the Brethren. They attribute their children's 'backsliding' entirely to them, failing to entertain the possibility that their own parenting regime might have had something to do with it.

The Brethren magazines repeatedly advocate punitive child-rearing practices.[2,3] Following the wisdom of the book of Proverbs 13.24, a writer indicates the benefit of some form of corporal punishment, but draws the line at 'the rod'. Similar tight control is recommended in all matters sexual, in relationships with the political authorities, and in participation in the education system.

However, to single out particular areas of authoritarian control is to run the risk of missing the main point: the overall culture of the tight Brethren is authoritarian, and the issue of authority permeates their lives. And the ultimate authority from which all belief and practice stem is the Bible. The primacy of the Bible's authority is the root belief of the Brethren culture, and it is to its detailed consideration that the next chapter is devoted.

Summary
This chapter uses the Question and Answer feature of Brethren magazines to explore the extent and form of authoritarianism found in the assemblies. The questioners appear to be only too eager to submit to authority, indicating that assembly believers are authoritarian in culture, not merely compliant in behaviour while harbouring secret dissent. They are, on the contrary, anxious to learn how they might more closely follow Assembly Truth: the supposed New Testament blueprint for assembly practice. They are also eager to discover how non-conformists should appropriately be punished, not only for biblical sins but for errors that offend the questioner. Authoritarianism is finally evident in the willing acceptance of the authority of the self-appointed overseers in assembly matters, and in the exercise of coercive parental control within the family.

NOTES

1. Editorial, *Precious Seed*, May 2011.
2. Davidson, J.A. Family Life: Discipline. *Assembly Testimony*, May–June 2015.
3. Paterson, J. Jnr. Relationships in Proverbs: Parents and children. *Assembly Testimony*, May–June 2013.

CHAPTER 10

The Authority of the Bible

THE ROOT BELIEF

The fundamental question for all religions is this: How does the transcendent make contact with humankind, and conversely, how does humankind make contact with the transcendent? Considering the monotheistic religions only, this question translates into the following: How does the transcendent God, who is, by definition, omnipotent, omniscient, and eternal, make Himself (or Herself) known to humankind, which has none of these three attributes?

As far as the Brethren and other conservative evangelical Christians are concerned, the answer to this question is clear. It can be expressed by the root belief of their conceptual system: *God speaks to people by His Word, the Bible.* In order for this to be expressed in action, a belief about value has to be added: We must obey God, and therefore we must obey His Word.

This root belief has been reiterated by Brethren, often eloquently:

For, behind the Writings, at that beginning, is the Lord – Jesus Christ – Himself. Nearer to Him, historically, we shall never get.[1]

The book, as a whole, and in every fragment, is a message from God. It comes to us with as real an intention as if it came with the direction of our name upon it, fresh from heaven.[2]

The Bible is given to us as knowledge: faith and obedience turn it into power.[3]

© The Author(s) 2018   89
P. Herriot, *The Open Brethren: A Christian Sect in the Modern World*,
https://doi.org/10.1007/978-3-030-03219-7_10

So perfectly does the Bible express the nature of God that its attributes reflect those of the Almighty Himself. God is omnipotent, and therefore, by definition, His Word must be completely *sufficient* for our needs. God is omniscient, so the Bible cannot make mistakes: it is *inerrant*. And God is eternal, implying a Word timeless and *universal* in its meaning and interpretation. Indeed, so closely are God and His Word identified that the Bible is often personified as though it were the Almighty: 'The Bible says...', 'the Bible commands...', 'the Bible requires...'.

These attributes of the Bible are inferred by Brethren from the root belief itself. For if God speaks to people by the Bible about Himself, then the Bible will tell us about His Word—about itself. It tells us that it is *sufficient:* "Man shall not live by bread alone, but by every word that proceedeth out of the mouth of God"[4]; that it is *inerrant:* "thy word is truth"[5]; and that it is universal and *timeless:* "For ever, O Lord, thy word is settled in heaven"[6]; "Heaven and earth shall pass away, but my words shall not pass away".[7] Brethren frequently quote proof texts, although generally by way of illustration.

SECOND-LEVEL BELIEFS

So, the sufficiency, inerrancy, and universality of the Bible constitute the second level of the belief system, following immediately from the root belief itself. With them, of course, come some immediate implications. If the Bible is *sufficient* for all our needs, then we have no need for any other of the social systems which constitute our late-modern world. No need, then, for science or politics or philosophy or organization or history or art or media.

In an article entitled "Building Your Library: Puritans and Poets",[8] readers are warned:

> Please note: although titles with an asterisk are specially recommended, the most important volume in the Christian's library is the Bible. All other books, however highly esteemed or recommended, must be checked against the one infallible book........ John Milton's *Paradise Lost*, is an astonishingly powerful if flawed attempt to turn the story of the Fall into epic poetry.

Paradise Lost was not asterisked.
And again:

> The faith is contained in the Bible as we have it handed down to us. To attempt to add to it or readjust it or to issue additional decrees as if they were of divine authority is to impugn the perfect work of the Holy Spirit and to be guilty of presumptuous impiety.[9]

Indeed, since the Bible is *inerrant,* any other accounts which appear incompatible with the Scriptures must be wrong, whether they are scientific or historical or whatever authority they claim. Their authority is fallible, derived from fallen Man, whereas

> there is no suspicion whatsoever of error or mistake in the facts, histories, doctrines, or affirmations of any part of the Bible. Man was created from the dust of the earth, the Garden of Eden was a fact, Noah's flood swept across the globe, Israel walked dry-shod across the Red Sea, the walls of Jericho fell flat, and Jonah was swallowed by a great fish![10]

And finally, what are the implications of the *universality* and timeless quality of the Bible? The result is that Brethren treat "the text as suspended from its authorship and speaking on its own".[11] If God is speaking to His people down the ages, then He would not address His Word solely to those for whom the biblical authors thought they were writing. On the contrary, He has made it comprehensible to everyone, regardless of their culture or location in history. It is the Almighty who is speaking to us, not the mere mortals whom He used to transmit His truth. They, of course, were tied to their time and place, but the Word is eternal.

Again,

> [i]t's safest to take words in their natural sense.....If Scripture doesn't mean what it says, how can we hope to know what it's about? The moment we abandon the literal sense, we are adrift in a sea of indeterminacy where no two interpreters think alike.[12]

And again:

> Never forget: God says what he means and means what he says. The Bible is not a book of coded mysteries to be explained only by some priestly elite. God graciously conforms to the conventional rules of human language and grammar.[13]

> We should never read our own ideas into the text. Let scripture speak for itself.......We need to always diligently compare scripture with scripture, allowing the Bible to interpret itself to us.[14]

Thus all idea of human agency and human difference is ruled out. The biblical writers were simply God's channels for transmitting His Word. Their contemporary readers were humankind no different from us today. Reading is a passive, receptive process rather than an active, sense-making one. The meaning is the same for everyone, and everyone can understand it, for God's Holy Spirit reveals it to them. Simply pray, read, and wait.

The Brethren's sectarian history suggests, however, that one Brother's clear meaning easily morphs into another's heresy.

THIRD-LEVEL BELIEFS

The implications of these beliefs about the Bible are profound indeed. They result from people who are living in the late-modern era treating premodern writings as God's words spoken directly to them. They consequently adopt the premodern world view which the biblical writers held.

The most central feature of such a world view is the very frequent attribution of events and actions to supernatural causes. Premodern people had relatively few alternative explanations available for events which they found difficult to understand, since their social world was not differentiated out into the various social systems of modernity. Modern people have a far greater choice. Each of today's differentiated systems offers one sort of explanation for particular types of event or another. Religious explanations are only one of several sources of explanation, and tend to be used in specific situations, for example, those which inspire wonder and awe.

The use of a premodern narrative to explain their own experience has, unsurprisingly, some profound consequences for the beliefs of tight Brethren. They fully embrace a view of history which considers past, present, and future to be already determined by the will of God. Indeed, Brethren have been advised not to vote in general elections because God has already determined the outcome. It is therefore a waste of time to exercise a vote, since the result has already been ordained. Further, if one votes for the losing side, one will have gone against the will of the Almighty.[15]

Moreover, their world is inhabited and influenced by a variety of supernatural beings: angels, demons, spirits, Satan, and so on. It is constituted of different places: earth, heaven, hell, and 'the air', and movement between these places occurs miraculously, as in the ascension of Christ and the rapture of believers. And as I have already remarked, asses and serpents speak, the latter in a real Garden of Eden, created by the Lord Himself.

The consequences of this continuous attribution to the supernatural put Brethren on a collision course with science, and in particular with theories of evolution.[16,17] Their view of history as a sequence of encounters with God alienates them from historians. And their view of humankind as afflicted by the inherited curse of original sin directly contradicts the Enlightenment narrative of human progress. It is hardly surprising that they feel aliens in a strange and hostile land.

It is worth stressing the absolutist nature of the idea of original sin. To quote:

the sin of every man today may be traced up to its polluted source in the disobedience of our first parent, Adam, in paradise. His sin was against the commandment of God (Gen. 2.17), and our sin today is still a disobedience and rebellion against that same Creator God and His holy law. When Adam sinned, he sinned as the father and representative head of all his race, and his sin therefore affected all his descendants. Sin's effects were carried like a poisoned stream from Adam down through the following generations of mankind, polluting and ruining the race. Today we are all, without exception, not only sinners by our inherited nature, but sinners by practice and choice.

Now, for most Christians

> The Bible as history went the way of the Bible as science and gave way to the Bible as myth. Myth was thought of not as error but as symbolic theological truth.[18]

But not by the Brethren. For them, defending the Bible as sufficient, inerrant, and universal is not a matter of defending a mere book. They are defending God Himself.

IMPLICATIONS FOR ACTION

Given the tightly organized and absolutist nature of the Brethren belief system, it is hardly surprising that their actions are equally absolutist. They are nothing if not consistent. They live in the spiritual sphere as God's Church, and therefore have nothing to do with this all too carnal world. They are the only believers who maintain the true New Testament model of the Church, and therefore the assemblies have nothing to do with 'the sects'. Man is by nature sinful, and therefore needs rescuing by earnest evangelism from the fires of Hell. History is determined by God, and there is therefore no point in seeking to make the world a better place. God moves in mysterious ways, so it is of little use to plan, organize, and reason. And God the Father exercises male authority, so we too should maintain the patriarchal authority of the Brother over the Sister—of which more in the next chapter.

Thus the root belief of the Brethren—that the Bible is God's Word to them, which they must obey—leads inexorably to a series of derived beliefs. These, in turn, separate them from the modern world, of which they apparently refuse to be a part. Yet, as I will argue in Part IV, they are, in effect, defined by the very world from which they constantly assert their distance: they are its diametric opposite. But first, we must address the question of what sort of head covering sisters should wear in the assembly.

Summary

The Brethren belief system is easily the most important element of their culture. It is organized in three levels, the root belief being that the Bible is God's Word to the believer. At the second level are other beliefs about the Bible: that it is sufficient, inerrant, and universal in its application. As the Word of God, it expresses His nature in these respects. At the third level is a whole range of beliefs which follow from its premodern origins. It attributes events to supernatural causes, it treats history as predetermined, it has a multi-level cosmology, and it considers truth to be absolute and given by revelation. From this system of beliefs, a wide range of implications follows for practice. Most important is withdrawal from the modern world as a means of separation from evil. In a binary world view, everything of human origin is evil.

NOTES

1. *Christian Brethren Research Fellowship Journal*, 1977, vol. 14, *passim*.
2. McIntyre. D.M. Bible knowledge. *The Believer's Magazine*, September 2012.
3. As 2 above.
4. St Matthew ch4 vs4.
5. St John ch17 vs17.
6. Psalm 119 vs89.
7. St Matthew ch24 vs35.
8. Newell, D. Building your library (xii) Puritans and Poets. *The Believer's Magazine*, July 2014.
9. Vine, W.E. The sufficiency and finality of Scripture. *Precious Seed*, vol. 12, no. 5, 1961.
10. Browne, M. Fundamentalism and the message of the Gospel (3). *The Believer's Magazine*, August 2008.
11. Lawrence, Bruce (1989) Defenders of God: The Fundamentalist Revolt Against the Modern Age, p. 115. Columbia SC: University of South Carolina Press.
12. Newell, D. Occasional letters: Apocalypse Now. *The Believer's Magazine*, January 2015.
13. Newell, D. A series of letters on Bible study (4) Recognising the genres. *The Believer's Magazine*, November 2008.
14. Taylor, Ian. The health, wealth, and prosperity gospel. *Precious Seed*, November 2014.
15. Question Box. *The Believer's Magazine*, September 2015.
16. Lawrence, op. cit. p. 173ff.
17. Campbell, Ian. Creation evangelism. *Precious Seed*, November 2005.
18. Browne, M. op. cit.

CHAPTER 11

The Authority of the brother

The Theology of Headship

The lowercase letter 'b' in the title of this chapter indicates that its primary concern is with gender. The titles of Chaps. 2 and 3, by way of contrast, have the letter capitalized. They cover the world views of the tight and loose factions of the Open Brethren, respectively. There is no chance whatever that 'sisters' could feature in these titles, since the words Brethren (for the sect) and brethren (for the gender) are practically synonymous. Only brethren could represent the Brethren.

So, what is the sister's place? To quote a sister's obituary[1]:

> After the death of her much-loved husband G, she continued as before, devoting herself with renewed vigour to that sphere of service allotted to Christian women: hospitality, encouragement of younger believers, private prayer. Many a young man and woman owe much to her unobtrusive ministry. She had a love for God's Word, especially the truth of the Lord's return for His saints, and an intelligent spiritual discernment superior to that of many men. But she never pushed herself forward, being content to fill her Scriptural place.

It is tempting to locate the tight Brethren's attitude to women simply as the automatic outcome of their treatment of the New Testament letters of St Paul as a rule book for how assemblies should function. This would, however, underestimate the extent to which authoritarianism permeates the sect. Rather, male 'headship' is embedded deeply in the belief system which directs and motivates the Brethren.

© The Author(s) 2018

P. Herriot, *The Open Brethren: A Christian Sect in the Modern World*,
https://doi.org/10.1007/978-3-030-03219-7_11

Authority derives, in this system, from the authority of God, who has determined the course of history from the Creation onwards through to His future final rule. God's authority is expressed to Man through His Word, the Bible, which the godly believer obeys. In 'natural' terms, Adam was created first, whereas Eve transgressed first and tempted Adam.[2] In spiritual terms, however, in the present Church dispensation, the Church is Christ's bride.[3] Christ is the head of the Church, and it submits to His headship. In its practice, the Church mirrors this divine order, with the brother exercising headship and the sister submitting to his authority. Submission to headship is symbolized by sisters covering their heads in the assembly.

If this appears an abstruse set of ideas, consider one example of how it worked out in practice. Early in the development of the loose Brethren faction, a progressive brother was concerned not only about the silence of sisters in the church, but also about traditional attitudes of men towards women. He wrote to 30 elders known beyond their own assemblies regarding the matter, and reported that

> [t]here was a certain reluctance to debate the matter, varying from pure indifference to active opposition to any discussion at all. The elders of the Assembly which I attend wrote to me not to press my views either in public or in private, adding 'We, as elders, consider it your duty to submit to us in this matter'.[4]

Clearly, authority is a sensitive issue. This last example exemplifies the dynamic nature of the influence process. Yes, the silence of sisters in assembly meetings is the outcome of their complex belief system permeated by the theme of authority. But equally, it is a practice conformed to because of the exercise of authority in enforcing that belief system. It is both an action of believers in accordance with their beliefs, and a conformist reaction to social pressure from others. But the progressive brother's initiative indicates the possibility of innovations being envisaged by an individual.

Change is indeed possible, and many assemblies have changed beyond recognition since my father's day. The assembly in which I was brought up and he officiated as elder has called itself 'Evangelical Church' since the 1970s, and is affiliated to the Evangelical Alliance. It employs two staff—the pastor (male) and a pastoral and youth assistant (female). All four elders are still, however, men. Such change is not primarily as a result of challenging *authority*. Rather, it has come about because of a dismantling of some of the cornerstones of the barrier of *separation*. The difficulty with challenging authority is its deeply embedded belief system. Any challenge can be portrayed as a challenge to biblical authority and therefore to God Himself.

Since *sola scriptura* is the root belief of the conservative evangelical wing of the Christian faith, it is not just 'Assembly Truth' which is being undermined but the very foundation of the (evangelical) faith.

This is clear from the attempts of loose Brethren to debate such issues as male headship and sexual orientation. These revolve around the interpretation of the key biblical passages used to justify these positions.[5] The assumption that the often ambiguous admonitions of St Paul to various groups of Christians in the premodern era should be read as detailed directions to late-modern Christians is rarely challenged. That would smack of heresy.

SISTERS IN THE ASSEMBLY

Tight Brethren consider the counter-cultural nature of their practices regarding women as an indication of how effectively the assemblies are separating themselves from 'the world' and 'the sects'. Consider Miss Boggs. A brother recalls his education at primary school at the hands of this brilliant and inspiring teacher. Yet, however articulate, she was silent in the assembly. "So I learned at a young age the difference between the ordering of things in the world, in contrast to God's assembly".[6]

And what was that ordering? It was designed to ensure submission to male headship.[7] Women, of course, are priests, in accordance with the principle of the priesthood of all believers. It is just that they are priests with different functions to men.[8] They provide hospitality, invite people to gospel services, teach the young, care for people with problems, and generally "add fragrance to the worship".[9] They can indeed pray, but they must do so in silence.[10] They cannot pray aloud even when no men are present, as there is no biblical justification for holding assembly meetings open only to certain (e.g. female) categories of believers.[11]

The key symbol of sisters' submission to headship is head covering, which must be worn in any assembly meeting, wherever it is held.[12] And mere ribbons or lace coverings are simply not good enough.[13] Any assembly breaking the rules regarding sisters' silence and head covering "is not truly a New Testament assembly".[14] Such assemblies are fighting against the truth of headship—they are "the workers of falsehood".[15]

BROTHERS, SISTERS, AND MARRIAGE

Male headship is not required only in the assembly, however. It should also be the guiding principle of believers' marriage.[16] But this, alas, is far from the case in today's fallen world.

"Fifty years ago in the western world," an American brother writes,[17] "typical family life was quite predictable and Biblical. From an early age, parents trained their boys to assume masculine responsibilities, and their girls to pursue feminine concerns. If there was free time, boys played with boys, and girls with girls. When a young man matured and was ready to marry, he courted a young woman, and eventually proposed to her – if he had her father's permission. During their engagement, the couple kept company only in public, because everyone expected them to act with honour and remain chaste until their wedding night. Their marriage created a stable nuclear family – a husband and a wife and their children formed the central 'nucleus' of church and town and nation".

And woe betide them if she asks him rather than the reverse, for this breaks the principle of headship.[18] She must not put temptation in his way by wearing revealing clothes, since men are only too easily aroused by the sight of uncovered female flesh.

Although David was answerable for his sins, Bathsheba may have been guilty of exposing herself to a man of God and bringing about his downfall. Women professing godliness should be aware that men are sensually aroused through sight, and therefore should avoid exposing too much of their anatomy.[19]

The female archetype of Eve the temptress seducing helpless men is dominant here. The story of the Garden of Eden suggests that women, having destroyed innocence, are to be ashamed of nakedness, not proud of it.[20]

Rather, throughout courtship a couple must discuss the Scriptures together to ensure they are of one mind, particularly with respect to male headship. "Thus it would be appropriate that very early in courtship stories of conversion would be shared and convictions regarding the assembly explored".[21]

This heterosexual ideal is, naturally, incompatible with any hint of homosexuality. There is no such thing as a gay Christian,[22] and gay marriage is a contradiction in terms.

It is clear from these scriptures [Genesis 19. 4-7, Leviticus 18. 22, Romans 1. 26-27, and 1 Corinthians 6. 9] that God does not create a person with homosexual desires. A person becomes a homosexual because of a sinful nature and ultimately because of his or her own choice.[23]

Such sexual relations are illicit. Anyway, homosexual couples obviously cannot observe the principle of male headship, and so the natural and God-given social order cannot be maintained, and gender roles are irretrievably confused.

AUTHORITY AND SEPARATION

The degree of female submission described in this chapter is one of the most distinctive features of the tight Brethren. It distinguishes them from 'the world', where the feminist movement has had immense success; from 'the sects', where women are ordained; and from the loose Brethren, where they pray aloud in public and fail to cover their heads. For the tight Brethren, sisterly submission is an absolute: a line in the sand which they will not cross.

A definitive feature of a sect is that it has separated from a larger religious system, usually a denomination or a movement. In the case of the Open Brethren, the separation was from a reformist movement within the Christian denominations. But the most obvious characteristic of sectarianism is its absolutism. There is only one body of truthful belief, and that is its own. Every other belief is in error, according to the tight Brethren, especially when it runs counter to 'Assembly Truth'.

When the authority for the belief system is the common sense reading of Scripture, the proliferation of sects is guaranteed. One man's common sense is another's heresy. This apparently was the case when the Brethren movement split into the Open and Exclusive sects in 1848. Two powerfully charismatic brothers are reported to have disagreed, among other things, about the interpretation of a prophetic passage of the Bible.[24] The two sects later differentiated further, the Open Brethren into tight and loose factions, the Exclusives into numerous further sects, at least one of which is now a cult.

It is this process of differentiation which drives the separation central to the Open Brethren, and especially to its tight faction. As I have argued already in Chap. 5, differentiation necessarily requires separation from other social systems which might be mistaken for one's own, and which are competitors in the same religious arena. The tight Brethren are particularly critical of the loose Brethren, since confusion and competition with them is very likely.

In Part III, I will first re-emphasize the close relationship between sectarian boundaries and social identities. Then I examine the tight Brethren's separation from 'the world', other Christians, and the loose Brethren faction. I will argue that the psychologically dominant form of separation of these three is from 'the world', since it is 'the world' which, they believe, has infected 'the sects' and also the loose faction of Brethren. Parts II and III are intimately related, since it is beliefs and practices about authority which inform and justify separation and sectarianism. However, the two parts are also psychologically distinct, in that authority is primarily to do with belief systems and conformity, whereas separation is bound up more specifically with identity.

Summary

The complex belief system of the Brethren places them in the present Church Age, when the spiritual relationship of the church with Christ is paramount. This relationship is expressed as one of marriage, with the church as His submissive bride. Church practice should reflect this relationship, they assert, and so the sister should be submissive to the brother, and cover her head in the assembly as a symbol of his headship. This belief in male headship is reinforced by St Paul's admonitions to early churches that women should remain silent in the assembly. It is further reinforced by the strongly counter-cultural nature of these beliefs and practices, since the worldly criticism they arouse indicates that the Brethren must be right. Lurking in the shadows are the premodern archetype of woman as Eve the temptress, and the fear of sexuality it expresses. More generally, patriarchal attitudes to women are typical of premodern societies. They are simply another example of assumed authority justified by reference to the Bible.

NOTES

1. With Christ. *The Believer's Magazine*, May 2013.
2. Question Time. *Precious Seed*, November 1947.
3. Question Box. *The Believer's Magazine*, June 2009.
4. Letters. *Christian Brethren Research Fellowship Journal*, vol. 14, 1962.
5. *Christian Brethren Research Fellowship Journal*, vols. 27, 1975 & 33, 1982 *passim*.
6. Arbuthnot, Stephen. Distinctions in Service. *Precious Seed*, May 2013.
7. Hay, J. Why I believe that sisters should cover their heads in assembly gatherings (2). *The Believer's Magazine*, May 2010.

8. Scammell, Peter. Women priests: An ecclesiastical debate. *Precious Seed*, May 1995.
9. Question Time. *Precious Seed*, November 2011.
10. Oakes, Mike. The assembly prayer meeting. *Precious Seed*, February 2015.
11. Question Box. *The Believer's Magazine*, July 2016.
12. Question Box. *The Believer's Magazine*, November 2007.
13. Summers, A. New Testament symbols, Paper 6, The head covering, Part 2. *Assembly Testimony*, September/October 2013.
14. Question Box. *The Believer's Magazine*, April 2008.
15. McBride, Samuel. The local church and its conflict. *Assembly Testimony*, 2008, Book 3, ch 12.
16. Campbell, J. Headship (continued). *Assembly Testimony*, November/December 1980.
17. Vallance, D. Christian apologetics (3): Marriage (1). *The Believer's Magazine*, July 2012.
18. Brown, D. Christian courtship. *The Believer's Magazine*, February 2010.
19. Gibson, J. The first epistle to Timothy: Praying, dressing, and teaching (1 Tim 2). *The Believer's Magazine*, March 2012.
20. Browne, M. Dress for Christians in today's world. *The Believer's Magazine*, October 2007.
21. Brown, D. (op. cit.).
22. Beck, Gordon. The biblical viewpoint of sexual relationships. *Precious Seed*, vol. 62, issue 2, 2007.
23. Coles, Howard. What does the Bible say about same-sex marriage? *Precious Seed*, vol. 62, issue 4, 2007.
24. Grass, Tim (2006). Gathering to his Name: The Story of the Open Brethren in Britain and Ireland, ch 4. Milton Keynes: Paternoster.

PART III

Separation

CHAPTER 12

Separation and Identity

MODERNITY AND DIFFERENTIATION

The essence of modernity is the differentiation of the social system. In the late-modern world, we have a wide variety of functional social systems, some of which are now global in their scope. One social system is differentiated from another by its primary purpose, its beliefs, values, and norms of behaviour, and its forms of communication. All social systems consist essentially of their communication networks and the social relations which these make possible.[1,2]

By late modernity, many of these global systems—for example, business, religion, and science—have themselves become extremely internally differentiated. They have expanded and branched out into new areas in pursuit of their primary purpose (to create wealth, to appreciate the transcendent, and to increase knowledge, respectively). As a consequence, they also have to spend time and effort ensuring a degree of systemic integration. Boundaries need to be drawn and conformity enforced to keep all the new subsystems firmly within the parent system. Threats to the system in the case of business, religion, and science would include, respectively, financial instability, heretical proselytizing, and methodological error.

The late-modern world is consequently characterized by highly developed social systems intent on growth in pursuit of their own main purpose, and also on control to maintain the system's integrity. Their self-contained and specialized character makes inter-systemic dialogue and collaboration increasingly difficult. Such relationships as those between

© The Author(s) 2018
P. Herriot, *The Open Brethren: A Christian Sect in the Modern World*, https://doi.org/10.1007/978-3-030-03219-7_12

business and science, business and government, and religion and culture are nevertheless established and maintained because each party needs what the other can bring in order to better achieve its own main purpose. But even these self-interested relationships are not easily conducted.

Given this system specialization, most modern people involved in a particular communicative system—for example, religion—will communicate within that system, limiting themselves to its basic aim and its beliefs, values, norms, and practices. They will not tend to engage in mixed modes in an effort to communicate with other systems. Rather, they will stick to using the communication mode specific to the system in which they are currently operating, be it religion, politics, science, or business. Of course, they are likely to be engaged in several social systems, but usually at different times and in different situations.

So, for example, Evangelical Christians will concentrate on enlarging the religious system by attracting more adherents. Neuropsychologists will spend most of their time adding to our knowledge of how the brain is related to behaviour. Investment analysts will seek to increase wealth by channelling capital into profitable business ventures. All of them will be communicating within their own social system so as to enhance the achievement of their primary aim. For most, their participation in a social system is almost entirely limited to communication with others within the same system.

For some, however, communication with people from another system will be frequent: investment analysts seeking to fund potentially profitable neuropsychological research, for example, or bishops trying to influence government's social policies. Much such inter-systemic communication is likely to be collaborative, as the participants perceive themselves to be in a win-win situation. Some of it will be hostile, however, as when two or more sets of beliefs, values, and practices appear incompatible and threatening. This has often historically been the case, for example, for religion and science.

THE WORLD, THE FLESH, AND THE DEVIL

But it is very hard to think of any social system which is hostile to all or nearly all of the other systems. This is because all systems are, to a degree, inter-dependent in the total global social system. They have differentiated out and developed precisely because they each contribute functionally something unique towards the integrated social whole.

However, a few such hostile subsystems exist, and one of them is the tight Open Brethren. As far as they are concerned, every other social system is to be avoided and shunned, unless it is an authority they believe God has told them to obey. This hostility is due to the constitution of the sect as a fundamentalist reaction against modernity itself. In premodern times, at least in Christendom, the only developed systems were religion and aristocratic power, usually in tandem. It is no coincidence that the authority of God and of rulers is the only authority which the Brethren acknowledge.

But it is not just all the other global social systems which they avoid and criticize. It is also every subsystem within the religious system apart from their own. The other global systems are forbidden because they are of human, rather than divine, origin. Since 'Man' is, by nature, evil, these systems are evil because they are 'of Man'. But even the religious system itself has been infected by the other systems. 'The world' has infiltrated 'the sects', defiling the purity of the bride of Christ, the New Testament church, with worldly organization and hierarchy and ritual. We Brethren, and only we, remain pure and undefiled, the faithful remnant.

But we are not even the remnant any more. No, we are but a remnant of a remnant,[3] for Satan has wheedled his evil way even into the Open Brethren ourselves. The so-called progressive brothers are apostates and heretics, infected by the spirit of this present age, and even more to blame because they have consciously rejected the truth which they know.

SOCIAL RELATIONS AND EMOTIONS

Thus, for the tight Brethren, 'the world' constitutes a generalized Other, an out-group that includes everyone except themselves. This enables them to stereotype the Other in terms of sin and shame, and to define themselves as not the Other. They themselves do not stand for sin and shame but for salvation and purity. They have to shun 'this world', except for purposes of evangelism and gospel witness. Staying resolutely and judgmentally outside, they venture in only in order to rescue the perishing.

This theme of *separation* revolves around social relations, in contrast with the theme of authority, which is concerned more with belief systems. Admittedly, the effect of the social group is apparent in ensuring conformity to authority, but in general, my analysis of authority was more in terms of cognition than of emotion. In fact, my psychological description of belief systems reflects conservative evangelical theology and the historical accounts of the development of the Brethren movement.

But separation is about social relations, a more obviously emotive arena. The nearly unique feature of the tight Brethren is their rejection of every other social system as tainted with human invention and therefore sinful. Other social systems are unnecessary, since the Word of God is *sufficient* for every need. Where another social system, for example, science, is incompatible with the *inerrant* Scripture, then it is, by definition, wrong. And since worldly systems have been developed subsequent to the writing of the Bible and the beginning of the Church Age, they cannot be *universally* and timelessly true. Hence, relations with these systems must be in terms of the superiority of spiritual truth over worldly error.

Given this absolutist position, there is no possibility of a dialogical relationship between the tight Brethren and any other social system or subsystem. Dialogue requires open minds to listen to and consider each other's communications. Rather, the only possible social process is one of incorporation of individuals into the tight Brethren on the latter's terms.

And those terms do not only involve separation in the active sense of leaving one system and joining another, 'coming out'. They also imply remaining secluded and pure behind the Brethren boundary walls thereafter, emerging only to evangelize. This interesting duality suggests that supreme confidence in one's own rightness is mixed with a strong fear of being defiled, seduced away by Satan's wiles.

Sure enough, 'the world' is often defined as that arch-enemy, Satan. To quote:

> ...the world, used in its New Testament moral sense, forms part of a kind of trinity of evil opposing the Holy Trinity, in which the world is opposed to God the Father, the devil is opposed to the Son of God, and the flesh is opposed to the Holy Spirit........It is clear, therefore, that Christians today need much wisdom in relating to the evil system of the world around them, since, although its structure was originally good and made by God, it is not in this age characterised by God, but rather by Satan, the evil one. Hence the need for principles to follow in our daily pathway of faith through the enemy territory around us.[4]

Fear of Satan's wiles, however, can often be accompanied by reassurance when we are persecuted by 'the world'. We must naturally expect the world's hatred and rejection, which parallels its hatred and persecution of Christ.

Ease and comfort in this present life are not necessarily a sign that we are rightly related to the world. It may mean that we have adopted worldly attitudes and compromised in our testimony to the world around us.

So we may have to actively terminate relationships which we have formed with the unsaved (the Other).

> Unconverted companions have been the means of leading many young believers back to the world. Make a clean cut with your worldly companions and associates if you want to go on with God. You cannot possibly have communion with God and with the world too.[5]

Rejection of friends on the basis that they might corrupt us, and then taking reassurance from their subsequent understandable 'persecution' of us, are the inevitable social and emotional consequences of the construction of everyone else as the evil world.

SOCIAL RELATIONS AND SOCIAL IDENTITIES

Social relations, I have previously argued in Chap. 5, are internalized and represented in the mind in terms of social identities.[6] Tight Brethren have developed an identity in terms of not being of this evil world, the Other. That evil world consists, in sociological terms, of all the other social systems than religion, and all the other religious subsystems than the tight Brethren. The Brethren's rejected 'world', then, is actually the source of most people's range of social identities. A single individual may construe themselves as Conservative, English, gardener, estate agent, music lover, football supporter, Roman Catholic, and so on. All of these identities are unavailable for the tight Brother. In fact, the only identities permitted are assembly believer, and a constellation of role identities associated with assembly fellowship, such as (dominant) husband or (submissive) wife, father or mother, assembly overseer, and so on.

The identity of 'assembly believer', therefore, has to bear a tremendous weight in the self-concept of the tight Brother. It will be salient in the mind in every social situation, regulating relations with the saints and 'the world' accordingly. There is only one choice of relationship possible: love, acceptance and conformity with the saints, and avoidance, rejection, or evangelizing of 'the world'.

The emotional outcomes of these forms of social relation are equally stark.[7] Acceptance by and affiliation with the saints will be accompanied by feelings of certainty and assurance that one is right; feelings of warmth and affection given and received; and high self-esteem and pride in being a member of God's select remnant of faithful believers. Avoidance, rejection, or evangelizing of 'the world', on the other hand, can be accompanied by feelings of anxiety in case one is defiled, self-righteousness, and superiority. And hatred of sin can sometimes translate into feelings of disgust at, and repulsion from, the sinner, rather than the love enjoined by Scripture.

And more generally, threats to assemblies or believers anywhere are a threat to me personally if my central social identity is that of assembly believer. Or, conversely, opposition to, or persecution of, the Brethren anywhere may simply confirm my own self-attributions of faithfulness and righteousness.

The overall consequence, then, of reducing social relations to tight Brethren versus everyone else is a parallel reduction in the complexity of the self. The believer's self-concept is reduced to one dominant social identity. This identity of assembly believer, together with the powerful emotions which it arouses, serves to direct and inform his or her actions in any social situation, however inappropriately. These actions are motivated and accompanied by a relatively small but often strong set of emotions. The tight Brother or Sister is thus extremely limited in their capacity to play many of the roles expected in late-modern society. They are likely to find themselves in difficulty communicating within systems other than the religious system, despite the daily social requirement of being capable of operating within several.

Modern humankind has complained about 'the divided self', the number of different social identities which one has to juggle. How, we may ask, can we maintain any degree of personal integrity while playing so many different social roles daily? The tight Brethren have a simple but impractical answer: avoid them.

Summary
The tight Brethren have become so differentiated from other social systems that they have lumped all these together into a single huge Other: 'the world', in Brethren parlance. The world, according to the Brethren, has infiltrated the churches, with the result that they now constitute 'sects'. These reflect Man's sinful pride in thinking that the simple model of the New Testament church can be improved upon. The world has even, allege

the Brethren, seduced some of the Open Brethren away from Assembly Truth. The consequence of this extreme differentiation is a siege mentality of fear of defilement, with the only reassurance being the experience of 'persecution'. The simple world view of Us, the true remnant, versus the Other leads directly to a simple social identity which is inadequate to deal with the complexities of modern life. The only solution is to separate from it and avoid it.

NOTES

1. Castells, Manuel (1996) The Rise of the Network Society. Oxford: Blackwell.
2. Beyer, Peter (2006) Religions in Global Society. Abingdon: Routledge.
3. McBride, Samuel. The local church and its conflict. *Assembly Testimony*, 2008, Book 3, ch 12.
4. Davis, Malcolm (1990) The Christian and the world. *Precious Seed*, 41, 5.
5. Danger Areas: A word for young believers (from Focus on Separation, by John Ritchie Publications). *The Believer's Magazine*, October, 2008.
6. Otten, Sabine, Sassenberg, Kai, & Kessler, Thomas (eds) (2009) Intergroup Relations: The Role of Motivation and Emotion. Hove: Psychology Press.
7. Laing, R.D. (1990) The Divided Self. London: Penguin.

CHAPTER 13

Pure from the World

THEOLOGICAL JUSTIFICATION

The belief system underpinning the tight Brethren culture is the obvious place to try to start understanding their obsession with separation and purity. And within that system, a crucial distinction is that between the fifth historical dispensation of the *law* given to God's *earthly* people Israel and the present *church* dispensation, where believers constitute God's *heavenly*, spiritual people (see Chap. 2).

The duality between the carnal and the spiritual is fundamental here. The earthly, or carnal, cannot have a pejorative connotation in the historical sense, since it was God Himself who chose Israel to be His earthly people. But it certainly gains one when believers are contrasted with unbelievers. For "[a] Christian belongs to Christ, the unbeliever to the Devil (this may seem strong language but it is true)".[1] And the Satan uses their carnal and earthly desires to seduce the saints, with the result that

> whilst having a poor appetite for the things of God, many have a prodigious appetite for the things of the world, friends, position, pleasure, and so on..........the world is to Satan his lure for the unwary Christian....Satan has little further interest in the professing Christian when he has made him spiritually dead, blind and deaf.[2]

But Christ is the glorified Man in Heaven, not in this satanically dominated world. The believers, as His heavenly bride, the Church, belong in

© The Author(s) 2018   113
P. Herriot, *The Open Brethren: A Christian Sect in the Modern World*,
https://doi.org/10.1007/978-3-030-03219-7_13

Heaven too. However, they are still temporarily placed here on earth, and still subject to the natural appetites of their earthly bodies and sinful human nature. Thus, believers tread a "daily pathway of faith through the enemy territory around us".

The world view implied by these theological beliefs is thus starkly binary. The earthly and carnal 'natural man' is corrupted by the Satanically organized world system.

> The trouble is that the heart has a bias towards evil, and has depths of motivation that God alone knows. 'The heart is deceitful above all things, and desperately wicked.........'. (Jer.17.9)[3]

Meanwhile, the 'spiritual man', Christ's pure bride, is constantly in danger of being seduced by the world, due to his retention of this corrupted earthly existence. The concept of what it is to be a human being is thus split right down the middle between spiritual purity and carnal vice, virgin and whore. The implications for the self-concept, for psychological integrity, and for mental health are profound.

But their powerful belief system is a convincing justification and a strong motivation for fundamentalist believers. It provides them with a world view which meets their needs for meaning and for direction, and for a sense of self-worth. These rewards seem to them to be worth their constant struggle against the world, the flesh, and the devil.

A Social Explanation

There is, however, another perspective from which we may view this struggle for purity. This is not an alternative explanation, simply an additional one. It derives from the need for the sect to differentiate itself from its competitors so as to attract—and above all, retain—its adherents.

As described in Chap. 4, the tight Brethren are concerned about losing adherents to the loose faction and to other Evangelical churches. The loose Brethren promote a wide range of heretical and dangerous compromises which they are happily making with 'the world'. They openly express their appreciation of the value of secular education, rationality, and science.[4,5,6] They advocate social involvement, in particular with regard to the disadvantaged.[7,8] They even suggest that art and culture can reveal God's greatness in creation.[9] And they point out that from the very beginning of the Brethren movement, there has been disagreement about the appropriate extent of believers' involvement in government and politics.[10] Why, they even begin an obituary of one of their number with a reference to his 'worldly' achievements.[11]

With their closest competitors advocating and practising this degree of worldly involvement, the tight Brethren had no option but to differentiate themselves. They had to offer a superior and purer faith, a more exclusive and meritorious spiritual identity. They had to become the remnant of the remnant.

Their first response was to point up the possibility of unworthy motivation in these activities. All of them could, of course, be motivated by the desire to witness to and convert sinners. Souls could indeed be saved by teachers witnessing to receptive minds; by scientists revealing the wonders of creation; by carers of all sorts demonstrating God's love in action; by artists pointing people towards the transcendent, and so on. And is not the salvation of souls the greatest commission with which our Lord charged His church?

But perhaps these involvements in the world are motivated by other aims than saving sinners, suggest the tight Brethren. Perhaps these more worldly believers are searching for acceptance by friends, or admiration for their own achievements, or gratitude from those they help, or reputation in the world at large. Perhaps they want to feel important or virtuous. All these motivations are temptations from the Satan. His wiles are subtle, and young believers in particular are vulnerable to his assaults. Rather than risk such vulnerability, then, avoid the danger in the first place.

And so a list of dangerous places is provided: friendship; entertainment, culture, and sport; work and politics; and finally, anything intellectual or professional. But the really dangerous place for the tight Brethren was the attractive evangelical church down the road with its crowds of youth, its raucous music, and its trendy young pastor.

UNEQUALLY YOKED

Young Brethren are cautioned:

> Be ye not unequally yoked together with unbelievers: for what fellowship hath righteousness with unrighteousness? And what communion hath light with darkness?........Wherefore come out from among them, and be ye separate, saith the Lord, and touch not the unclean thing; and I will receive you. (2 Corinthians 6. 14 & 17)

Unconverted companions have been the means of leading many young believers back to the world. Make a clean cut with all your worldly companions and associates if you want to go on with God. You cannot possibly have communion with God and with the world too......This sort of association can easily arise when believers are away from home for the purposes of study or in the pursuit of employment. They can then be lonely for human companionship, and may even feel that Christian fellowship is lacking in their new location.[12]

So the godly family and the home assembly are the only really safe places for the young believer. When these are left behind as the believer becomes an adult, perils abound. The Brethren are only too aware of these possibilities. When I left home to go to Oxford University, an eminent brother from the local assembly came to college to invite me for Sunday service and lunch. When I married and moved to Northern Ireland, the same thing happened, but on this occasion, another eminent brother was too late. We were already away, off to the Methodist sect!

The safest thing to do when you enter a new study or work environment is to witness.

When you go for the first time into a new situation let your testimony be clear. It will save you much trouble later, and keep you from being sucked into compromising associations.[13]

So witnessing keeps you safe as well as saving souls. And saving souls is the only legitimate reason for associating with unbelievers.

The main reason for avoiding friendships with unbelievers seems to be the social activities which these friendships usually entail. "Do not be blind", young believers are advised, "to the dangers of entertainments, amusements, and clubs, even religious ones. Evening parties or day outings, where believers and unbelievers are associated, are not really for those who wish to walk with God. Loose language, social drinking, carelessness, frivolity, and flirting all take place under the guise of outings and amusements in the world". And

the lust of the flesh, and the lust of the eyes, and the pride of life, is not of the Father, but is of the world. (1 Jn 2.16)[14]

INTELLECTUALS AND PROFESSIONALS

While the flesh is an ever-present temptation, the mind is just as danger-ous, if less obviously seductive. And where is intellect and reason more dangerous than in the university? Various disciplines are selected out as particularly harmful to the Brethren student: English, modern languages, religious studies, geology, philosophy, and politics.[15] The reasons for their singling out as a particular threat can only be speculated upon. Brethren students are advised to join the local assembly and beware the Christian Union, which may be Charismatic. And they should not get any inflated ideas: "the possession of a degree should carry no weight among the peo-ple of God".[16] On the contrary, there is too much emphasis on academic and professional qualifications in the assemblies.[17]

This suspicion of academics and professionals is doubtless related to the need to differentiate the tight Brethren from the looser faction. The latter were more likely to be suburban middle-class assemblies with a greater number of adherents of this type. But it also follows from a fundamentalist view of biblical sufficiency, and a refusal to acknowledge the authority of any other than the religious social system. In particular, it reflects the tight Brethren rejection of the fruits of the Enlightenment and the benefits of the arts and science.

Two medical examples illustrate this rejection. The first is that of a brother suffering from depression. His family doctor

> sent a psychiatrist to our home. He took one look at my Bible on my arm-chair, Christian books in my bookcase, and texts on the walls, and announced that this was my problem. He told me I had 'religious mania'. We had a strong conversation.[18]

The brother lost his job, but carried on reading his Bible and preaching, and ultimately recovered from his depression.

The second example is the preference of many Brethren for homeo-pathic medicine.[19] As Tim Glass suggests, homeopathic treatment is often chosen and administered by patients themselves. It may therefore indicate mistrust of professional knowledge, and rejection of the overwhelming empirical evidence showing that homeopathic treatment has nothing more than the placebo effect.

POLITICS AND SOCIETY

Many fundamentalist Christians, particularly in the United States, are heavily involved in politics.[20] The rise of the Moral Majority in the 1980s and the New Christian Right in the 1990s and early 2000s involved campaigning on the basis of a few key 'moral' issues, such as abortion, divorce, homosexuality, and home schooling. Christians voted for candidates who supported conservative positions on them, and held them to account. These movements have had profound effects on the culture of American politics and government, although liberal legal provisions generally remain in place. The tight Brethren, on the other hand, have been consistently hostile to political involvement or indeed to political participation of any sort.

Once again, one level of explanation for this difference points to a difference in belief systems, in particular on the topic of eschatology. In brief, Brethren hold a pre-millennialist position, to the effect that Christ will come to rapture believers before the millennium. Many American Protestants, however, are post-millennialist, believing that they can hasten God's rule by their efforts in the world on His behalf. Indeed, extreme elements such as the Constructionists preach the establishment of theocratic rule.[21]

More generally, however, avoidance of politics is an obvious example of the general Brethren principle of separation. Given that the political system is a key element of the world system defiled by Satan, there is every reason to shun it. In this respect, the tight Brethren resemble that stream of fundamentalist belief which seeks separation and purity rather than involvement and struggle. The Amish are a transatlantic example of this separatist strand.[22]

The tight Brethren position has been summarized thus:

> Christians are not directed to improve the world but to proclaim the gospel that condemns it and offers salvation from it. Financial contributions to political parties, participation in election campaigns, running for political office, and voting are all activities which constitute an unequal yoke with unbelievers.[23]

There is nothing more important than preaching the gospel to an alien world:

> Having known salvation, we now are pilgrims moving towards another destination and strangers in a land which is not our home. The task which falls to us is to preach the gospel and to display the Lord Jesus to a world lost in sin. Great though the issues of the day may be, there is none greater than that.[24]

So we must concentrate on the spiritual and eternal rather than the carnal and temporal. All we are enjoined by Scripture to do in the world is to obey the authorities who have been appointed by God, pray for them, and pay our taxes. Any greater involvement in the affairs of this world than this would compromise our witness and put us in danger of sin.

> There is danger when Christians aspire to positions of power in the world because they expose themselves to the world's corruption, its thinking, and its sin. (see 2 Tim 2.4)[25]

And there are further dangers to the individual and the assembly. If believers vote, they might find themselves voting for someone whom God has not appointed, and thus be disobeying His will. And further, the assembly might become divided.

> Voting for a particular candidate would be sure to provoke discord among the people of God who, if all were to vote, would certainly not 'be of the same mind' (Phil 4.2), 'of one accord' (Phil 2.2), and 'all speak the same thing'. (1 Cor 1.10)[26]

No, Western politics is not for the saints. For

> (t)he essence of democracy is rejection of any notion of absolute truth or higher authority and rejection of absolute values through acceptance of the rightness of whatever the majority think. This is anti-scriptural.[27]

It is in their opposition to 'the world' that the tight Brethren demonstrate most powerfully one of the characteristics of fundamentalism: its duality. Their world view distinguishes the spiritual and the carnal, the sacred and the secular, the heavenly and the worldly, with complete mutual exclusivity. This world view is represented in their self-concept: they are saints, not sinners; saved, not lost; believers, not unbelievers. Thus they can personally identify with the virtuous binary alternative.

Summary
The tight Brethren world view contrasts carnal 'natural' man with spiritual man. Believers, of course, constitute the latter category, but have to beware the lingering seductive power of the former. This emphasis provides a differentiation which can attract and retain adherents, permitting them a self-perception of greater purity from the world. To achieve such a

level of purity, believers must become separate from all other social relationships except those within the family and the assembly, the only safe havens. Social relationships are compromised by the temptations of the flesh, but often more dangerous are the temptations of education and professional status. This high level of separation distinguishes the Brethren from most other fundamentalist movements, which practise a degree of involvement in politics.

NOTES

1. Coles, Howard (1998) The Christian and the World. *Precious Seed*, 53, 3.
2. Howell, J.D. (1974) Separation from. *Precious Seed*, 25, 1.
3. Coles, op. cit.
4. *Christian Brethren Research Fellowship Journal*, vol. 7, The Church and Education.
5. *Christian Brethren Research Fellowship Journal*, vol. 19, Science and Faith.
6. *Christian Brethren Research Fellowship Journal*, vol. 3, The World, The Flesh, and the Devil.
7. *Christian Brethren Research Fellowship Journal*, vol. 35, The Caring Church.
8. Summerton, Neil (2012) The 'big society', integral mission and social action: some reflections and concerns. *Partnership Perspectives*, Summer.
9. Martin, C.G. *Christian Brethren Research Fellowship Journal*, vol. 18, Applications.
10. Wilson, Elisabeth (2004) Your citizenship in heaven: brethren attitudes to authority and government. *Brethren Historical Review*, 2, 75–90.
11. Rowdon, Harold, & Grass, Tim (2012) Obituary: F. Roy Coad, 1925–2011. *Brethren Historical Review*, 8, 100–104.
12. *Precious Seed*, May 2010. We're getting married: Help and advice please.
13. *The Believer's Magazine*, October 2008. Danger areas – a word for young believers.
14. *The Believer's Magazine*, April 2010. Question Box.
15. *Assembly Testimony*, May/June 1992. Higher education.
16. *Assembly Testimony*, July/August 1992. Higher education.
17. *Assembly Testimony*, March/April 1985. Losing the power of the Holy Spirit by degrees.
18. *Precious Seed*, May 2016. Depression: A personal experience.
19. Grass, Tim (2006) Gathering to His Name: The Story of the Open Brethren in Britain and Ireland. Milton Keynes: Paternoster, p. 257.
20. Lienesch, Michael (1993) Redeeming America: Piety and Politics in the New Christian Right. Chapel Hill NC: University of North Carolina Press.

21. Herriot, Peter (2009) Religious Fundamentalism: Global, Local, and Personal. London: Routledge, pp. 131–2.
22. Hood, Ralph, Hill, Peter, & Williamson, Paul (2005) The Psychology of Religious Fundamentalism. New York: Guilford, ch 6.
23. Cooper, K. Why I believe that Christians should not be involved in politics. *The Believer's Magazine*, August 2011.
24. Grant, J. What about politics? *The Believer's Magazine*, April 2015.
25. Cooper, op. cit.
26. Question Box, *The Believer's Magazine*, September 2015.
27. Cooper, op. cit.

CHAPTER 14

Separated from the Sects

A Foundational Feature

A historical appreciation of the Brethren is, of course, vital to understanding their present condition. However, in no aspect is this cliché more true than in their relationship with 'the sects', that is, other Christian denominations and movements. From the very beginning in the 1820s of what started as a movement, the Brethren have stressed their dissatisfaction with other Christian institutions.[1]

Their original complaint appears to have been the compromises which the then current leadership of the Church of Ireland was making with what they called 'Romanism'. Several clergy of the Church of Ireland were in the process of seceding from it, or had already done so. While the initial emphasis of the movement was to receive and worship together with all 'true' believers, it soon started to distinguish itself from the doomed 'visible' church. Influenced strongly by the prophetic passages of the Bible, Brethren characterized the denominations as defiled by the Satan. His apostate agents, they alleged, had associated the established church with the state; they had added unscriptural elements in violation of *sola scriptura;* and their rituals had inhibited the inspirational action of the Holy Spirit.

Their immediate origins thus set the Brethren movement on a strongly anti-establishment course. The split of 1848 resulted in two sects—the Open and the Exclusive Brethren. The latter, under the leadership of J. N. Darby, sought to exercise a central control over assemblies. Partly in order to differentiate themselves from this centralizing tendency, the Open

© The Author(s) 2018

P. Herriot, *The Open Brethren: A Christian Sect in the Modern World,*
https://doi.org/10.1007/978-3-030-03219-7_14

Brethren emphasized by way of contrast the autonomy of each assembly. This was another stimulus for separation from the denominations, since, of course, some form of organizational structure and direction is characteristic of all denominations. Thus the 'spiritual' nature of each assembly, under the authority and direction of the Holy Spirit, was contrasted with the sinful and worldly authority of 'the sects' controlled by Man.

This construction of reality continued to be used, despite the various methods of communicating between assemblies and with missionaries which gained popularity, such as magazines, conferences, and so on. From the beginnings of the Open Brethren, then, the autonomy of each assembly was an expression of the opposite of two Others, the denominations and the Exclusives.

Further historical developments soon followed. Particularly in Scotland and Northern Ireland, Open Brethren experienced hostility from the denominations. This was in response to what were perceived as proselytizing activities seducing away church members. This was frequently achieved by revivalist preaching of a simple gospel of salvation which attracted working-class people.

The result was that, particularly in these areas, Brethren were more hostile to the denominations in response. When such interdenominational activities as the Billy Graham evangelistic campaigns occurred in the 1950s and later, the strength of this sectarian hostility resulted in condemnation of the participation of mainly English Brethren. The mostly suburban Southern English supporters of collaboration with the denominations were thus set against their provincial, mostly working-class counterparts. These structural and historical roots of the tight and loose factions nourished the open conflict described in this chapter.

PURE AND SIMPLE

In answer to the question in the *Precious Seed* Question Time 'Which church should I join and why?',[2] the respondent lists no less than nine alleged characteristics of churches in New Testament times, as follows: They had no sectarian title; no earthly headquarters; contained no unbelievers; were guided by overseers; instructed by various preachers; permitted no audible female participation; celebrated the Lord's Supper weekly; met for prayer; and preached the gospel.

The questioner is advised to search out such a church (i.e. a Brethren assembly). It is the only church which "abandons all man-made ecclesiastical systems, and identifies with the rejected Christ". The main reason why such a church reports to no central authority is to safeguard against false teaching, for

> If the devil infiltrates a central authority, false doctrine will then be pushed out to every congregation in the group to become a compulsory creed for all.

The key idea here is the habitual binary distinction between human and divine action. 'Ecclesiastical systems', that is, Christian denominations, are 'Man-made', whereas the assemblies are the work of the Holy Spirit alone through the Word of God. The assemblies, therefore, are pure in doctrine and practice, since nothing human (that is, impure) has been involved in their formation and continuation.

This purity is threatened, however, by any contact with Man-made, and therefore impure, systems, or their representatives. To descend from the lofty theology of W. E. Vine[3] to a more earthy metaphor,

> in Christendom the core is rotten even though the outside looks good to eat, while in the assemblies the core is right but the outside is sometimes unattractive. But.....you can clean up a dirty apple but you can do nothing about a rotten one.[4]

So, anything which, or anyone who, can possibly introduce impurity into that apple of God's eye, that bride of Christ, the assembly, has to be excluded. Collaboration with the sects in evangelistic efforts is obviously out of the question.

> It is important to see that it is from the assembly that the gospel should go forth.....This is the divine pattern......the winning of souls should be with a view to converts progressing to baptism and reception into assembly fellowship.[5]

After all, some evangelical groups do not teach (adult) baptism or the truth of separation from the world.

Practices of the denominations should also be avoided, even when collaboration is not involved. City Missions, for example, are used by the forces of spiritual evil

> "to deceive assemblies into embracing that which has an appearance of good but which is in reality evil".[6] These are "projecting an apparently non-sectarian image and holding a place at the very forefront of good works and

evangelical endeavour in many of our cities". But they are "outside the scope of God's New Testament pattern and therefore designed to overturn divine principles and divide the saints".

Indeed, all such denominational activity by assembly believers is wrong. It takes time and energy away from the assembly's work; it confirms the denominations in their own error when they see believers fraternizing with them; it compromises fundamental doctrinal principles; it causes disunity in the assembly; it weakens the credibility of the believer who engages in it; it leads to conflicts of loyalty; and it dishonours the Lord Jesus Himself.[7] In sum, it does not have too much to commend it.

Little wonder then that, to return to the metaphor above, the outside of the Brethren apple is often unattractive. And little wonder too that while the loose Brethren appear not to be losing too many adherents, the tight Brethren are haemorrhaging assemblies as well as members.[8]

KEEP CALM AND CARRY ON

So what is to be done? There is only one conceivable response from within a closed and absolutist belief system: continued faithful obedience to the Lord's commands. To quote:

> Although God's pattern for gathering is increasingly unfashionable, our duty is to maintain it through thick and thin, faithfully serving the local assembly in which He has placed us.[9]

And

> [w]e should not use the decline in numbers to become a pretext for unscriptural change and the compromising of Scriptural standards and the Biblical pattern. The honour of Christ's name must take priority over all other considerations.[10]

For some fill churches by pleasing Man, but we have a completely different objective: to please God.[11]

The good old days can still come back again:

> So let's think of those amazing times when God revived His work in our country and thousands were saved at vast evangelistic campaigns. Well, thank God for such memories! We were there, and it was real. Now let's believe He can bring it back again.[12]

Can we not find once more the grace to yield afresh all that we have to the altar of Christ? There is yet time to prove Him the Saviour God that He is. Let's do it![13]

It is worthwhile at this point recapitulating the psychological underpinnings of this refusal to contemplate any change in belief, values, or practices. The tight Brethren do not engage in any detailed prediction of when exactly the Lord will return, satisfying themselves with the observation that the signs of the times and the ever-increasing depravity of the world suggest that this longed-for event is imminent. However, their attempts to explain their predicament are reminiscent of the famous occasion in the USA '*When Prophecy Failed*',[14] and the world carried on much the same as usual. How do believers cope with any clear disconfirmation of their beliefs?

The answer appears to be that they apply other elements of their belief system to help them to explain their disappointment.[15] In this case, the tight Brethren expected to be blessed by God with an increase in adherents as a result of their faithful preaching of the gospel. However, their efforts failed to yield the expected converts. On the contrary, assemblies are closing and adherents deserting.

Now the tight Brethren cannot change any aspect of their core belief system, which specifies not merely their central aim of saving souls, but also the means by which this is to be accomplished (gospel preaching). To abandon any aspect of their tightly structured system would be to put their entire social identity at risk, since for the Brethren their belief system is the core of their identity. This is why the magazine authors quoted earlier urge them to continue with their faithful obedience to Scriptural practice. There is no other course of action possible. What they can do, however, is adduce other reasons for their plight which are derived from their belief system. Explanation will firm up the system in the face of such disappointment, and give them justification and motivation for carrying on.

The doctrine of separation provides an ample source of such explanations. In the overall Brethren world view, matters relating to the assembly come into the spiritual, rather than the natural, realm. Consequently, attributions of responsibility for assembly decline are likely to be to spiritual entities, in this case Satan. Satan has polluted the world, providing many alternative attractions to the gospel. He has infiltrated the denominations, adding human organization and ritual to God's pure and simple Scriptural plan for the church. And he has even seduced some assembly believers— the enemy within—and persuaded them to subvert the divine pattern, as the next chapter describes.

Since the tight Brethren believe that the assemblies alone obey God's will in their beliefs and practices, there is no possibility of change. The only course of action open to them is to remain faithful and trust in the Lord to defeat the Evil one. This construction of reality enables them to maintain their culture intact and unchanging. Their identity as the righteous and persecuted remnant is secure, and the light of their hope of imminent rapture to dwell for ever with their Lord in heaven burns undimmed.

But this security needs defending, and the ramparts firmed up. No practice typical of the sects, such as music, can be admitted,[16] for there is no Scriptural permission for it, and therefore it is of Man and not of God. To admit anything over and above what the Bible prescribes is "to move on a way that lies through ritualism to clerisy and priestcraft".[17] And no one from outside can be allowed in to Break Bread simply because they say they are a Christian. They have to bring a letter of commendation from another assembly to say they are 'sound' in belief and practice, or they have to demonstrate to the overseers that they are such.

Indeed, so important is the principle of assembly autonomy and purity that some forms of contact even with other assemblies, let alone with 'the sects', are dangerous. Pooling of resources, missionary support organizations, itinerant preachers, joint meetings, assembly magazines, assembly address books, internet forums, and so on could all be perceived as potentially compromising autonomy.[18,19] For these activities often constitute human organization typical of denominations.

No, the ideal is to stick to the local. Local duties should always come first,[20] especially attendance at assembly meetings.[21] In a word, keep calm and carry on being faithful.

Summary

Dissatisfaction with the mainstream Protestant denominations motivated the beginnings of the Brethren movement. They contrasted the control of the Holy Spirit in the assemblies, whereas the 'sects' were regulated by sinful Man's organization and hierarchies. The only way properly to submit to the Spirit's guidance was to ensure the independence of each assembly. Historically, relations with the 'sects' were strained, particularly in Scotland and Northern Ireland, where the Brethren were accused of proselytizing among mainstream adherents. In Southern England, however, collaboration often occurred within Evangelical circles. The emphasis on independence was justified in terms of the sanctity of Assembly Truth, as opposed to the unscriptural practices such as infant baptism and paid ministry practised by the 'sects'. Collaboration was certainly no solution to the decline in Brethren numbers, which was due to continued demonic infiltration of false teaching.

NOTES

1. Grass, Tim (2006) Gathering to his Name: The Story of the Open Brethren in Britain and Ireland. Milton Keynes: Paternoster.
2. *Precious Seed*, Question and Answer, August 2011.
3. Vine, W.E. (1959) Is the scriptural assembly possible today? *Precious Seed*, vol. 10, no. 4.
4. *Precious Seed*, vol. 61, no. 3, 2006. Are you still in fellowship? (anonymous).
5. *The Believer's Magazine*, August 2007. Question Box.
6. Laidle, W.L. (1987) The activity of spiritual evil. *Assembly Testimony*, January/February.
7. Coulson, D. (1986) Denominationalism. *Assembly Testimony*, March/April.
8. Brierley, Peter (2015) Independent churches – how are they doing? *Partnership Perspectives*, vol. 54, Autumn.
9. *The Believer's Magazine*, June 2013. Occasional Letters: Sticking to the pattern.
10. Cooper, K. (2014) Numerical strength in assemblies today. *The Believer's Magazine*, May.
11. *Precious Seed*, August 2011. Editorial.
12. *Precious Seed*, vol. 62, no. 2, 2007. Editorial.
13. *Precious Seed*, vol. 58, no. 4, 2003. Editorial.
14. Festinger, Leon, Riecken, H.W. & Schachter, Stanley (1956) When Prophecy Fails. Minneapolis: University of Minneapolis Press.
15. Spilka, Bernard, Hood, Ralph, Hunsberger, Bruce & Gorsuch, Richard (2003) The Psychology of Religion (3rd edn). New York: Guilford, pp. 356–360.
16. *The Believer's Magazine*, May 2011, Question Box.
17. Sweetnam, M. (2014) The church of God (4): The passion it declares. *The Believer's Magazine*, May.
18. Cooper, K. (2011) The autonomy of the local assembly (2) *Assembly Testimony*, September/October.
19. *Precious Seed*, November 2016. Question and Answer.
20. *Precious Seed*, vol. 60, no. 2, 2005. Editorial.
21. *Precious Seed*, vol. 56, no. 4, 2001. Question and Answer.

CHAPTER 15

Apart from the Apostates

Defending Identity

The main tactical task of sects is to differentiate themselves from other religious systems, and to maintain that differentiation as clearly and sharply as possible. If their key features are not distinctive enough, they will cease to attract and retain those for whom these features are particularly attractive. The Brethren *theological* distinctives are much discussed,[1] but reduced to their core elements they probably consist in the priesthood of all believers, the autonomy of the assembly, the centrality of the Breaking of Bread, and the return to New Testament simplicity in church order.

While these, taken together, constitute their distinctive character, there are other central theological beliefs which Brethren share with some other conservative evangelical movements and sects. The most prominent of these are the sole authority of the Bible, the substitutionary atonement of Christ, the imperative of evangelism, and separation from this evil world.

But what are the Brethren's *psychological* distinctives? They are, as I argued in Chap. 5, primarily concerned with identity. For many of the men who have influence in the tight Brethren, the identities available to their fathers and generations before them have disappeared. It is no longer easy to define oneself as the skilled and hardworking breadwinner and head of the family, and to have a respected position in a local community based on that identity. Uncertainty and unpredictability, and hence insecurity and anxiety about the future, have replaced the social, local, and

© The Author(s) 2018   131
P. Herriot, *The Open Brethren: A Christian Sect in the Modern World*,
https://doi.org/10.1007/978-3-030-03219-7_15

family status which they previously enjoyed. So has the weakening of the local and national social institutions which underpinned that status.

It is not difficult to understand how the assembly can provide a social system which offers alternative, but equally rewarding, identities. There are many roles, but especially those of overseer and preacher, which bring respect and status, albeit within a social micro-system. The uncertainties of employment and of social change are replaced by the certainty of belief. One knows that one is right with God and right about God: right *with* Him because, once we have been converted, we are assured of eternal salvation; and right *about* Him because He has revealed to us precisely how we should worship and serve Him.

However, the more the sect is forced to differentiate itself from other social systems, both secular and religious (Chaps. 13 and 14), the less possible it becomes for Brethren to hold other social identities. This is because the beliefs, values, and practices associated with the latter are incompatible with those of the increasingly central and dominant identity of assembly believer. And the more different and dominant the assembly identity becomes, the greater the need to defend it against dilution and infection. For it is one's self one is defending, as well as the true faith.

The worst danger of all now becomes not the wicked world itself, nor the worldly denominations, which are generally kept at arm's length. Rather, it is "the enemy within".[2] If we cannot feel secure even within the assembly ramparts, the very core of our being is threatened. For there is nothing left of our selves if the assembly goes. And this is why the greatest hostility is reserved for the loose faction, who are betraying us as well as what they know to be the Scriptural truth.

LOST DISTINCTIVES

The loose brethren are castigated for abandoning 'Assembly Truth', those distinctives which differentiate the Open Brethren from other sects. They are perceived to be attacking the very core of assembly belief and practice. They are "bringing a slow and sure pathway to a world of grey where no distinctions are to be drawn".[3] Little do they realize that they are the instruments of Satan himself, a scenario captured in the alliterative article titled "Spiritual Strengths Spoilt by Satanic Subtilty" [sic].[4]

The rot set in properly in the 1950s, when Brethren evangelism got mixed up with unscriptural associations and worldliness. The Christian Brethren Research Fellowship contributed further to the decline with their "subversive tendencies"[5] and Swanwick conferences. Their successor organization, Partnership, "remains a clear and present danger to the continued testimony of assemblies today in every part of the UK". While Northern Ireland and Scotland have resisted to a degree, the English assemblies have suffered most from their depredations.[6]

So how do these apostates infiltrate their falsehoods so successfully? Their first step is to sow the seeds of doom and despondency.[7,8] They prophesy decline and departure with every message they deliver, shamelessly pointing to younger men and women going to larger denominational churches. They bemoan the ineffective evangelism and the paucity of spiritual gifts in the assemblies. And having created this perceived problem, they craftily introduce so-called solutions, which actually serve to deny Assembly Truth. Arguing that the attraction and retention of young people is the key to survival, they foster discontent with the supposed neglect of this group by the overseers. They then try to replace or outmanoeuvre existing overseers in order to further their agenda.[9]

And what is that agenda? "Alien notions of worship – often tinged with a 'charismatic' flavour", together with participation and wider roles for sisters,[10,11] meetings for sisters only, worldly musical accompaniment, casual dress, and modernist versions of the Bible. But the challenge goes wider than the conduct of worship. For these apostates also seek to dilute Bible teaching on such issues as homosexuality and divorce. They breach the boundaries of separation from the sects and the world. Why, they even countenance such worldly diversions as theatres, cinemas, and dances. And they permit the youth to interact with unsaved friends on social media.

Danger lurks everywhere.

> Overseeing brethren who permit younger married sisters in the assembly to organise youth activities for young sisters in their teens and twenties need to be very careful as to what they are condoning. House meetings may spring up easily, but who is in control; who regulates what is taught; what other recreational or 'cultural' activities are promoted? To what kind of role model are these young believers being exposed?[12]

The desperate need to control everything that is going on in the assembly is clearly overwhelming. Obviously, what these sisters need is the wisdom of a man from the oversight.

So what is to be done to counteract these pernicious and insidious influences which are seeking to destroy the witness of the assemblies by undermining Assembly Truth? Since the Scriptures are completely clear as to what assemblies should believe and how they should practise their faith, any change is contrary to the will of God and bound to fail in the long run. Rather, Christ urges them to remain faithful and "hold fast till I come" (Rev 2. 25). Then they will share in His power and assist Him in administering retribution.[13]

Sound assemblies might be tempted to excommunicate assemblies which have succumbed to these temptations,[14] but this would be an unscriptural response. The solution is not "unscriptural separatism but Bible-directed separation".[15] This distinction is between assembly action ('separatism') and the action of individual believers, who are to distance themselves from heretical tendencies ('separation'). The discipline to be administered, at least to start with, consists of contention for the truth, resulting in the restoration of 'likemindedness'. Clearly, dialogue this is not. Rather, the saints should thank God if these apostates leave the assembly. No, the answer is to remain faithful and build up the defences against Satan's infiltration.

LETTERS OF COMMENDATION

One way to draw up the drawbridge is to ensure that those who enter the assembly to participate in the Breaking of Bread are sound in their support for 'Assembly Truth'. Letters of commendation are a mechanism to ensure that false doctrine and unrepented sin does not creep in. The following close textual analysis of an article in the *Believer's Magazine*[16] offers a window into the belief system underpinning the practice (my own glosses are in square brackets).

The first section summarizes in a series of bullet points the general principles regarding letters of commendation which a study of all the related Scriptures reveals. Their aims and purposes are first specified. They may be "an expression of spiritual unity" [an assembly may be greeting another 'likeminded' assembly]. They also "serve an important purpose in guarding the testimony [the assembly] from evil".

They should follow the following rules. They should not be a formality, or simply a matter of routine. On the contrary, they should be personal to the individual whom they are commending (or, possibly, not commending). They should be "positive, short, honest, and an accurate description of the person in question". And they should be justified by references to appropriate Scriptures.

However, the author stresses that letters of commendation are insufficient grounds for admitting those who are not already in fellowship into the Breaking of Bread. If the letters are the only evidence required, then visiting preachers or family members may get away without producing one. Moreover, we would be naive. For the assemblies writing a letter may not

> appreciate the significance of their actions, or set out the full information that would be pertinent to the receiving assembly. Sometimes letters are generated which do not convey the full facts. So, for example, one assembly may take a certain view on doctrinal matters (e.g. prophetic truth, truth relating to the person of Christ) or practical matters (e.g. divorce and re-marriage, recovery of an immoral person) which could be compromised by reception based on a letter from an assembly which takes an entirely different view on the matter.

No, letters are certainly not sufficient, given that there may be "circumstances or information known to receiving assemblies which make reception inappropriate despite the production of a letter". Equally, and for the same reason, letters are sometimes not necessary for reception to be granted, for example, for frequent visitors or preachers well known to the assembly. On the other hand, if such a person has not visited for some years, a letter "would be a good way of giving the receiving assembly confidence that in the lapse of time the person has not become uncommendable".

The overwhelming responsibility is on the receiving assembly, however. The overseers need to be careful that they are not receiving unbelievers; persons excluded from other companies [assemblies]; people who will hinder spiritual progress; and those who hold to false doctrine. Fuller enquiry which goes beyond the letter should be conducted where possible, a legitimate process which "no right-minded believer will resent". There are, for example,

> times when saints move from one assembly to another under unclear, unexplained, or unsatisfactory circumstances. The question might be raised as to whether a letter should be given in such circumstances. It should be recognised that there is a responsibility on those providing a letter to ensure that the wording does not misrepresent the position.

As if the problem of defending the assembly from long-term dangers is not difficult enough, we also have to consider holiday visitors.

"This can be a particularly difficult problem...Without any means of knowing the persons visiting, there is a great burden on the receiving elders.....
The elders have a responsibility to preserve the sanctity and order of the
assembly". The visitors might seek "to impose their own views", and demonstrate "a spirit which treats with contempt the requirements of that local
company" [assembly]. And they are certainly not on holiday from their
assembly duties, since "they should attend all the assembly gatherings con-
vened throughout the week, and not simply the Lord's Supper".

Some powerful themes run through this extraordinarily detailed article
dealing with a highly specific procedure. First, the fear of the faintest possibility of the contamination of assembly believers by 'false' doctrine is the
main motivation. Such a fear reveals a low estimate of the ability of believers to understand and weigh up anything for themselves. It also demonstrates once again the totally unshakeable confidence in the correctness of
the doctrinal position and biblical interpretation of the writer.

The article also demonstrates a considerable degree of mistrust.
Commending assemblies are not to be trusted to 'tell the truth' about a
person [assuming that there is only one truth, rather than different per-
spectives]. And holiday visitors are not to be trusted to treat the local
assembly with respect. Here are fellow believers who wish to worship God,
yet they are not welcomed but rather forced to negotiate an obstacle
course. Fear of the enemy within is indeed a powerful driver.

A Peculiar People

The Open Brethren are little known outside evangelical Christian circles,
and not even there are they prominent. They do not conduct public battles,
either in the ecclesiastical or the political war zones. Hence, they are unlike,
for example, the Calvinist movement in the Church of England, whose
aggressive campaigning has resulted in the popular misrepresentation of the
Anglican Church as a homophobic and misogynistic anachronism.[17]

As I will argue in the next chapter, the Open Brethren, notably in their
tight faction, are an archetypal fundamentalism. They exhibit all of the
defining features of this category of religious movement. However, they
follow the minority fundamentalist path of withdrawal and separation
from the evil modern world rather than the majority one of engagement
with, and hostility towards, it. Hence much of their activity is below the
radar, and the nature of their culture comes as a surprise to many (including,

doubtless, some of my readers). This is particularly true of their belief system, with its counter-cultural insistence on the supreme authority of a text and on supernatural explanations of events.

The choice of the Brethren as an archetypal fundamentalism has, I hope, drawn attention away from the inevitable current association of fundamentalism with violence and aggression. The Brethren are, rather, a perfect example of a social subsystem which is so differentiated within its parent global system (religion) that it has very little communication with any other religious subsystem, let alone with other global systems than religion. Almost all its communications are with itself. It is thoroughly self-referential. Its two dominant concerns are with its own practices and with gaining more adherents.

I will now argue in the last part of the book that the danger of fundamentalisms is not the violence which some few fundamentalists perpetrate, but the isolation resulting from their extreme differentiation. For no social system can survive if elements are almost entirely detached from it. And this is particularly true of our global social system, which depends upon a continuous interchange between the global and the local, between the integrated and the differentiated.

I will also argue that social systems and their interrelationship are dependent on their representation within the mind of their members. In particular, the simple self-concept of fundamentalists is dominated by their identity, in this case as assembly believers. This representation of self in the world is woefully inadequate to enable social systems to relate and achieve an equilibrium between differentiation and integration. If the religious and the other global social systems are to become sufficiently integrated, the self-concept of religious adherents needs to be complex enough to represent adequately such a level of integration.

Summary

Believers' identification with their assembly is central to themselves, and therefore, any threat to the assembly is a threat to the self. The most dangerous threat of all is the one nearest to home, from 'the enemy within', loose Brethren. These are accused of being prophets of doom, creating a false picture of ineffective assemblies and outdated practices. They offer unscriptural solutions to this non-issue which undermine Assembly Truth and foment discontent with the oversight. They can only be effectively kept at bay by careful control of who is allowed into contact with the assembly. Even letters of commendation for visitors from other assemblies are insufficient; additional sources of information must be consulted to ensure they are sound in doctrine and blameless in witness. The tight Brethren have, then, morphed from an open and optimistic movement to a fearful and defensive fundamentalist sect.

NOTES

1. Grass, Tim (2006) Gathering to his Name: The Story of Open Brethren in Britain and Ireland. Milton Keynes: Paternoster, chs 7 & 20.
2. McBride, Samuel (2008) The Glory of the Local Church: Chapter 12: The Local Church and its Conflicts. *Assembly Testimony Magazine*.
3. *Precious Seed*, 2009, vol. 64, no. 1. Editorial.
4. Avery, B.E. (2011) Spiritual strengths spoilt by Satanic subtilty. *Assembly Testimony*, January/February.
5. McBride, op. cit.
6. *Assembly Testimony*, January/February 1984. Editorial.
7. *Precious Seed*, 2003, vol. 58, no. 4. Editorial.
8. Summers, Alan (2016) How can I know which church is right? Questions young people ask. *Assembly Testimony*, January/February.
9. McBride, op. cit.
10. Sinclair, A. (2007) The message from the seven churches for today (5). *Believer's Magazine*, June.
11. Graham, H.W. (1999) "Stay in" or "Come out" WHICH? *Assembly Testimony*, November/December.
12. McBride, op. cit.
13. Sinclair, op. cit.
14. Currie, B. (1992) A consideration of lampstand removal. *Assembly Testimony*, January/February.
15. McBride, op. cit.
16. Cooper, Ken (2012) Letters of commendation (2) *Believer's Magazine*, May.
17. Herriot, Peter (2016) Warfare and Waves: Calvinists and Charismatics in the Church of England. Eugene OR: Wipf and Stock.

PART IV

Fundamentalism

CHAPTER 16

An Archetypal Fundamentalism

TRULY RADICAL

The Open Brethren are of little interest to the general public. They do not cultivate media attention, nor are they scandal prone. Their publications and websites appear to be primarily intended for their own consumption. The novels which have raised their profile, such as Edmund Gosse's classic *Father and Son* and Garrison Keillor's more recent *Lake Wobegon Days*, are no longer in fashion. It is, consequently, easy to ignore how extraordinarily radical they really are. Their absolutist belief system, their separate identity, and their counter-cultural world view are so unusual that they are difficult to comprehend for many late-modern people.

It is, of course, hard to discover how closely Brothers' and Sisters' individual beliefs and practices approximate to the Brethren prospectus, but some such shortfall is to be expected, given the latter's starkly uncompromising nature. In any event, we expect those with radical ideologies to propagate them aggressively and publicly in word, image, and action. When, like the Brethren, they fail to do so, we tend to ignore them, and so, fail to appreciate their truly counter-cultural nature.

So, to recapitulate, their religious belief system is *universal*. They believe it is applicable to every human being, to every age and culture, and to every situation. Truth is always *absolute*, never relative, and it is divinely revealed rather than discovered by humankind. Since it is universal and absolute, there is no point in engaging in dialogue about it: it is either obediently accepted or sinfully rejected.

© The Author(s) 2018
P. Herriot, *The Open Brethren: A Christian Sect in the Modern World*,
https://doi.org/10.1007/978-3-030-03219-7_16

The truth is easily received, as God has revealed it completely in His Word the Bible for everyone to read and understand for themselves. The Bible has total authority—it is God speaking directly to humankind. It is necessary, as it is the only way to discover Him. And it is sufficient to enable believers to live their lives in obedience to God's will. They have no need of any other source of knowledge to verify God's nature or His will for their lives. Rather, God's Word spells out in mutually incompatible binary terms the fundamental difference between God and Man, the spiritual and the worldly, good and evil.

This is, to repeat, the Brethren prospectus, but there are other conservative Evangelical Protestant movements and sects which would happily sign up to it. However, the proposition that the Bible is its own interpreter leads the Brethren to believe that what are really their own interpretations are God's truth, in such matters as ecclesiastical practice and eschatological prophecy. They, therefore, differentiate themselves from everyone who does not share these interpretations, thus following the historical Protestant tradition of sectarian division. To others, however, the Bible seems not to be so unambiguously clear after all.

This sectarian separation leads to a distinctive social identity for the Brethren as the only true believers. They are separate not only from this evil world, but also from other Christians, who have been seduced by Satan into disobeying the clear commands of God's Word regarding church belief and practice. True believers need to defend their boundaries to keep themselves pure from the spiritual wiles of Satan as well as from the worldly pleasures of the flesh. The consequence for their self-concept is that their view of themselves is dominated by their identity as a true (Brethren) believer. Everyone else is Other. The Brethren identity is salient in all aspects of their lives, and regulates their behaviour in every social situation.

This combination of their bounded religious belief system and their separate social identity results in the internally consistent but radically counter-cultural Brethren world view. If the reader is unfamiliar with the Brethren, they will have read the first chapter of this book in astonishment. However, to repeat, the Brethren world view is entirely self-consistent. It has an internal logic, once its initial assumptions are granted. But it also makes sense when it is viewed in the context of what Brethren believe they are up against: secular modernity.

MODERNITY

The Brethren themselves think and speak of modernity only in terms of their own belief system and language. This is all that they have available with which to describe what it is that they are fighting. Consequently, they refer to modernity in religious terminology as 'the world', or 'Man', or 'Satan,' or 'secularism'.

Social scientists, on the other hand, place at the centre of their definition of modernity the progressive historical differentiation of social systems from one another.[1,2] Religion, from this perspective, has by now become one of several separate global social systems, each with its own aims, values, and practices; and, crucially, each with its own criteria for deciding what is and what is not true.

In recent times, far more extensive differentiation has occurred. Religious movements and sects, having differentiated out from their 'parent' religion, each offer their own truth criteria, overlapping but differing in some particulars. Thus in the case of Christianity, mainstream denominations include the church, the Bible, reason, and spiritual experience as authorities for belief. They rely on these four authority sources in different proportions, with Roman Catholics, for example, giving greater authority to the church, and Pentecostals to spiritual experience. However, for all of them, there are several authorities.

The Brethren, however, recognize only one of these: the Bible. They are therefore differentiated not only from other social systems such as science or law or the arts, but also from nearly all other Christians. The recognition of all these other social systems, secular and religious, would dangerously imply that the truth is relative and specific to those systems rather than absolute and universal. And worse, that its origins and authority are human as well as divine.

Thus there could not be a greater contrast than that between the social scientific (and hence modernist) and the Brethren world views. For the former, the Brethren represent a highly differentiated social system at the edge of Christianity, itself a subsystem of the global system of religion. For the latter, they themselves are right at the centre of God's system—for they are His only true church.

But this is, of course, merely one example of the total incompatibility of the two world views. Every single aspect of the belief system and the social identity of the Brethren is the reactive opposite of modernity. As Bruce Lawrence puts it, referring to fundamentalisms in general, the core contest is between two incommensurate ways of viewing the world, one which locates values in timeless scriptures, inviolate laws, and unchanging mores, the other which sees in the expansion of scientific knowledge a technological transformation of society that pluralizes options both for learning and for living.[3]

We may therefore understand each of the world views not only from its own perspective, but also from its denial by the other. Modernity certainly does not depend for its meanings on the Brethren, although it is possible to understand it better by considering their view of it. But the same is not true of the reverse: the Brethren really do need modernity. For what else would they have to define themselves against? As many have already noted, fundamentalisms are themselves modern movements, in the sense that they are reactionary responses to modernity.[4,5]

To point up the polar opposites, first consider the two opposing views of the *nature of reality*. How are events and actions to be explained? For modern people, attributions of causality tend to be very varied. Explanations can be in terms of human motives or character, social situations, a combination of the personal and the situational, naturally occurring processes, or pure luck or chance.[6] For Brethren, however, attributions are generally to supernatural beings, God or Satan, or to religious concepts such as sin or redemption.[7]

Similar polarities are evident in the area of *values*.[8] In pluralist multicultural societies, the maintenance of social cohesion depends on a degree of communal tolerance for a range of value priorities and behavioural norms. Such tolerance requires the opportunity for dialogue, debate, and dissent, and the constant review of values and norms. For the Brethren, on the other hand, God's laws for belief and conduct have been revealed once and for all. They apply universally, and exist not to be debated but to be obeyed.

Modernity sees *the future* as being in our hands as humankind.[9] We are responsible for the survival of the planet and for the development of global society. If we continue the progress we have undoubtedly made thus far, there is no reason why humankind should not increase its well-being and realize its huge potential. On the other hand, we also have the capacity to destroy ourselves completely. For the Brethren, however, the future has already been determined by God. There is no point in seeking to influence what is going to happen, for only the Almighty's final judgement awaits. Our sole task is to live in faithful obedience to God in this wicked world and save souls for the next, until He comes.

World Renouncers

While the modern world has largely ignored the Brethren, they have treated it as their enemy. But how have they acted out this opposition? The researchers who completed the Fundamentalism Project[10] have characterized four ways in which fundamentalisms, in general, have sought to overcome their opponents. These types they labelled world conqueror, world transformer, world creator, and world renouncer. They differ immensely in how they act, but they share the same consuming hostility to modernity.

World conquerors seek to conquer the world for God by any means. If they succeed, the result is a theocracy, as in Iran. The nearest Protestant movement is Reconstructionism in the United States, which aims for biblical law to be established in the land of the free.[11] Given that the objective of this sort of fundamentalism is conquest, though not necessarily military conquest, those few fundamentalisms which favour violent methods are to be found within this category.

The second category is that of *world transformers*. These movements also intervene in the political process, but follow its rules when doing so. The Moral Majority in the United States, and later the New Christian Right,[12,13] are historical examples already quoted. They selected a few key 'moral' issues to contest through democratic elections, but have made relatively little progress on these restricted objectives. They have, however, gained considerable political influence in the process.

World creators seek not to transform the modern world, but rather to create a parallel spiritual world of their own, an enclave of God's faithful people set within an apostate world. They are eager to increase the size of this enclave by evangelism. Many Pentecostal sects, for example, fall into this category.

Finally, *world renouncers* reject the world as irredeemably evil and establish high boundary walls against it. They focus on internal purity, but ironically are often dependent on the freedom and resources of their host nation for their continued survival. The Amish in the United States[14] and some of the Jewish Haredim in Israel[15] are examples.

Where are we to place the Brethren within this set of fundamentalist categories? Indeed, are we justified in applying the much contested label of 'fundamentalism' to them in the first place, as I have done indiscriminately until now? In response to the first of these questions, we may argue that at the beginning of the Brethren movement in the 1820s, it was clearly a world creator. Its founding fathers sought a way of worshipping

God which better reflected the ideals of the early church, rejecting what they regarded as the compromised and formalized church of their day. Their concern was primarily spiritual and ecclesiastical—they were not interested in political activity. On the other hand, they did not avoid, but on occasion actively sought, charitable involvements. And they immediately set out to make converts abroad as well as at home.

However, the sectarian split of 1848 between the Open and the Exclusive Brethren, and the subsequent infighting in the Open Brethren between the traditional tight and the modernizing loose factions, suggest a more conservative core forcing the Open Brethren sect into a more separated and defensive posture. On the evidence of the previous 14 chapters, they might now be appropriately located as world renouncers.

Some Fundamentalists

From the first chapter, I have referred to the Brethren as fundamentalists without justifying this label. Of course, in one sense the category was lost as an analytic tool as soon as it became a term of media abuse for those responsible for terrorist acts. But the concept still has considerable purchase, for it may be applied justifiably to all religious movements and sects which define themselves in opposition to modernity. And as I will argue, fundamentalisms so defined are hostile to the development of the global social system by means of the development of relationships between its subsystems.

Without any doubt, the Brethren are radically fundamentalist. They are quiet, law-abiding, and peaceful people, but their world view is totally incompatible with modernity and with the globalization of society. They are, as they would say, and quoting the Bible as usual, 'in this world but not of it'. However, instead of further semantic argument about the use of the F word, this chapter concludes with a comparison of the Brethren with two other fundamentalisms, the Amish,[16] and the Calvinists within the Church of England.[17] Similarities and differences are evident regarding their belief systems and their posture towards the modern world, but they are united in their opposition to modern beliefs and values.

The Brethren and the Amish are both Bible believers, but the latter do not regard it as the only authoritative source of the truth. Rather, they supplement it with a charter detailing their beliefs and the wisdom they have derived from their long tradition. They also maintain a code of behaviour, the *ordnung*, which is oral rather than written and is adapted periodically to address issues raised by social or technological innovations.

The Amish pay a great deal of attention to behavioural norms and values, placing more emphasis on the gospel accounts of Christ's compassionate and humble actions than on the doctrinal emphases of St Paul or on the end-time prophecies. As did Christ, they concentrate on symbolic actions as a way of witnessing to the truth. The power of their symbolic actions to attract attention is evidenced by what they are primarily known for to the general public—their 'quaint' social customs. These, however, are not intended as traditional badges of membership or culture, but rather as symbols of their fundamental values. Horse-drawn buggies and sober dress are statements of a lack of interest or concern with individual social status and wealth, and as signalling humility and community. In their emphasis on humility and holiness expressed in action, they contrast with the Brethren, who are more concerned with doctrine, teaching, and preaching.

The second contrast with the Brethren is in terms of growth in numbers. The average size of an Amish family is around seven children. They only lose between 10 and 15 per cent of their children to 'the outside world'. This low rate of attrition is achieved by a high degree of separation, with children being withdrawn from school at US grade 8 and encouraged to work on the farm with their parents and siblings. Farming is easily the most popular Amish occupation. Separation itself is enforced strictly, with the ultimate sanction for involvement with the world being 'shunning', or total social exclusion. The tight Open Brethren, by way of contrast, are declining in numbers, at least in the UK. Despite their emphasis on separation, they lose many of their offspring, seduced by the ubiquitous media and lacking the pastures of the Midwest in which to hide.

But their similarities with the Brethren are also fundamental. Both aim for separation from the world (but only one largely succeeds). Both have been subject to sectarian schism (for the Amish, the Old Order Amish vs. the Mennonites). And both see themselves as the only true church:

> To this day, the Amish see the true church of Christ as a redeemed community called out and separated from the larger church, which has fallen from what God had originally intended.[18]

Amish and Brethren, therefore, both represent absolutism and separation rather than relativism and integration. They are world-renouncing fundamentalists.

The Calvinist movement within the Church of England, on the other hand, is not a world renouncer, but a world transformer. The transformation it seeks is primarily within the denomination of which it remains a part, but it also campaigns on issues of moral concern within British society. These are the perennial fundamentalist obsessions with gender roles and sexual orientation. So, for example, they have been tireless in their ultimately unsuccessful efforts to prevent the church ordaining women priests or promoting them to bishop. And they have repeatedly condemned homosexual acts as sinful and wrong for clergy in particular and Christians in general. They have also campaigned politically in support of those who have been sanctioned for disobeying legal or professional requirements in these areas. Examples are providing 'therapy' to gay people so as to change their sexual orientation, refusing to accommodate gay people in a hotel, or wearing a crucifix at work contrary to corporate directives.

They have succeeded in delaying the Church of England's acceptance of women and gays, and in gaining it a reputation for misogyny and homophobia. Apart from this reputational damage, they have also inflicted opportunity costs, as the church has had to spend much of its time and energy fighting internal political battles instead of addressing the important spiritual and moral issues in British society.

All of this denominational and political activity by the Calvinist movement is, of course, anathema to the Brethren. The former want to gain control of their denomination, while the Brethren dismiss all denominations and want nothing to do with them. The Calvinists court publicity, the Brethren shun it. But they both share the same conservative Evangelical belief in the Bible as inerrant, and in the doctrine of the substitutionary atonement through Christ's sacrificial death for our sins. And, like the Brethren, they are so absolutist in their beliefs that they dismiss their opponents as apostates and heretics, while they themselves are the only true remnant, in their case true to the Reformation. This results in their refusing to have any communion or fellowship with their Brothers and Sisters in the Church of England who are of a different persuasion. "We will not be robbed of our Anglican identity," they rage. "You are the usurpers. We will not allow you to deprive us of our Anglican heritage of faithfulness to the Bible".[19]

These comparisons of the Brethren with the Amish and the Calvinists point to the wide variations in the doctrines and practices of religious sects or movements which reject modernity. But they also point up the absolute centrality of that rejection, which is their very raison d'être. It is what enables us to apply the label fundamentalism to them all, and then to explore what they mean for religion as a whole and for global society.

Summary

The Brethren are absolutists: as far as they are concerned, there is one truth: God's revelation, which is available to all, but which only they have accepted. They are therefore a sect, but are they a fundamentalist sect? The definitive feature of fundamentalism is opposition to modernity, and this opposition is indeed central to Brethren culture. Because of their core belief in the Bible as the universal Word of God, their culture is incompatible with that of the modern world. This is because the essence of modernity is its differentiation into various functional social systems, each with its own culture. The Brethren cannot entertain such pluralism, with its belief in human progress, the acquisition of knowledge, and human rights. The modern and the fundamentalist world views are also incompatible with respect to the explanation of causality, the relativity of values, and the centrality of human agency. The Brethren response is to renounce the evil world and separate from it rather than attempt to change it. In this respect they resemble the Amish, but differ from such fundamentalisms as the Calvinists within the Church of England.

Notes

1. Beyer, Peter (2006) Religions in Global Society. London: Routledge.
2. Casanova, Jose (1994) Public Religions in the Modern World. Chicago: University of Chicago Press.
3. Lawrence, Bruce (1989) Defenders of God: The Fundamentalist Revolt Against the Modern Age. Columbia SC: University of South Carolina Press, p. 232.
4. Almond, Gabriel, Appleby, Scott, & Sivan, Emmanuel (2003) Strong Religion: The Rise of Fundamentalisms around the World. Chicago: University of Chicago Press.
5. Lawrence, op. cit., ch. 1.
6. Ross, Lee, & Nisbett, Richard (1991) The Person and the Situation: Perspectives of Social Psychology. New York: McGraw-Hill.
7. Taves, Ann (2009) Religious Experience Reconsidered. Princeton NJ: University of Princeton Press.
8. Bruce, Steve (2000) Fundamentalism. Cambridge: Polity Press.
9. Scholte, Jan (2005) Globalisation: A critical introduction. Basingstoke: Palgrave Macmillan.
10. Almond et al., op. cit.

11. Herriot, Peter (2008) Religious Fundamentalism: Global, Local, and Personal. London: Routledge, ch. 7.
12. Murray Brown, Ruth (2002) For A "Christian America": A History of the Religious Right. New York: Prometheus Books.
13. Harding, Susan (2000) The Book of Jerry Falwell: Fundamentalist Language and Politics. Princeton NJ: University of Princeton Press.
14. Kraybill, D.B. (2001) The Riddle of Amish Culture. Baltimore: John Hopkins University Press.
15. Heilman, S. & Friedman, M. (1991) Religious fundamentalism and religious Jews: the case of the Haredim. In M.E. Marty and R.S. Appleby (eds.) Fundamentalisms Observed. Chicago: University of Chicago Press.
16. Hood, Ralph, Hill, Peter, & Williamson, Paul (2005) The Psychology of Religious Fundamentalism. New York: Guilford Press. ch. 6.
17. Herriot, Peter (2009) Warfare and Waves: Calvinists and Charismatics in the Church of England. Eugene OR: Wipf & Stock.
18. Hood et al., op. cit., p. 140.
19. www.anglicanmissioninengland.org/amie-game-changer

CHAPTER 17

The Brethren and Modernity

A Critical Juncture?

So, the Brethren are important after all, despite their relative obscurity. They are important for what they are *not*: they are not violent, and they are not political. This makes them all the more important for what they *are*: an archetypal radical fundamentalist sect which directly challenges the beliefs, values, and practices of modernity. By studying the case of the Brethren in detail, we have cut to the essence of the fundamentalist world view.

But, we may argue today, the Brethren and all the other fundamentalists need not have bothered after all. It is fashionable to construe the current crisis in world politics as heralding the death throes of the modernist project.[1] Many millions across the world are currently dissatisfied with modernity because, as far as they are concerned, it has failed to fulfil its prospectus. A credible radical critique[2,3] of modernity's current neoliberal and individualist expression might run as follows:

In many nation states, modernity has stalled in its progress towards making each generation better off and healthier than the previous one. It has, instead, resulted in increasing inequality between the rich and the poor.[4] Even in the richest nations, it has allowed the continuation of large-scale abject poverty. It has degraded the quality and the security of work and employment. It has failed to control the speculative excesses of the finance sector, with potentially catastrophic consequences. It has allowed technological innovation to proceed at will without consideration of its possible downsides.[5] It has encouraged rampant individualism at the expense of social and civic bonds. It has ignored the interests of the local majority, promoting instead those of the global elite. It has permitted the subversion of democracy, destroying transparency and accountability, and collecting and using our personal information without our consent. And above all, it has threatened the longer-term survival of the planet as an ecosystem.

Now, many of those experiencing such outcomes might not sign up to this particular radical narrative. But they certainly appear to doubt the optimistic modernist vision of material progress and individual freedom. They are therefore willing to entertain alternative world views, one of which, authoritarian nationalist populism, is very attractive at present.[6] In such a pivotal historical context, fundamentalisms too offer a powerful authoritarian ideology, making the alluring but impossible promise to wipe out the modern era and take us all back to a golden age of purity and obedience.

It is, however, rashly premature to hail the long-predicted rise of postmodernism from the ashes of a failed modernity. This is because *the social systems underpinning modernity still remain largely intact and effective.* Differentiated global systems still continue to pursue their own aims, maintain their own value priorities, make their own assumptions, enforce their own practices, and hold their own world view. They still each apply their own criteria for deciding what is true. Business is still business, politics is politics, science is science, and religion is religion.[7]

What's more, there is a general recognition that this specialization will continue, despite populist politicians' vilification of experts. Not too many are as yet willing to accept the Foreign Secretary as their brain surgeon. It is not the differentiated structure of modern society that is generally held responsible for the present crisis. Rather, there is a widespread perception that key modern institutions and organizations serve the interests of those who own or control them rather than those whom they claim to serve. A democratic deficit in accountability and transparency is commonly experienced, and individual greed is more likely to be the motive attributed than the common good. 'The system', in sum, is felt to be working badly—but it still remains the system.

So the Brethren and all the other fundamentalists are right. Their enemy, modernity, *is* still alive, and if not in the best of health, is still kicking powerfully. The differentiated social systems which underpin it continue to flourish in the global environment. And they do so because they have, over the long term, resulted *overall* in vastly improved health and well-being globally.

At the present critical juncture for modernity, then, the following are among the key questions for discussion. In order of importance, first, *what impact is religion as a global system likely to have on the outcome?* Second, *how will fundamentalism affect religion's impact?* And third, *how are the Brethren involved in all this, if at all?* I will address them, I hope modestly, in reverse order!

AWAY WITH JESUS

Throughout my account of the Brethren, it has been clear that their actions are logically derived from, and completely consistent with, their theological beliefs. Their world view draws a rigid distinction between the spiritual and the material. In the present church dispensation, they live their lives at the spiritual level, avoiding this evil world. Every conceivable thing about this world is wrong: its politics, its media, its education, its art, its science, all of its institutions and organizations and movements. Yes, and even its Christian denominations.

All these are 'of Man', not 'of God'. God instructs the Brethren to obey the authorities and pay their taxes. But He certainly does not permit them to become involved in civic activities such as voting or trade union or professional memberships. Nor does He wish them to have friendly and social relationships with those who are not Brethren, except for the purpose of evangelism. And He warns them of the dangers of compromising the truth by collaborating with 'the sects'. This even applies to evangelism, Christ's great commission.

In their social isolation and spiritual purity, the tight Brethren differ from most other Christian fundamentalists. Fundamentalists are apt to form movements with specific social aims, usually *restorationist* ones. That is, they want to get back to the golden age when Christian family values characterized the nation, or when the Reformation zeal swept all before it in the church. Their aim is for a Christian America,[8] or a Reformed Anglicanism.[9] They are consequently—like it or not—necessarily involved in national or ecclesiastical politics, and with the media activities that accompany them in the modern world. They have to get organized.

The Brethren too are in favour of restoration. But they do not need to develop a movement to achieve it, for they are sure they have already succeeded in the task. The only restoration they want is that of the pure and simple New Testament local church, which they have already established. Let others compromise with this world. For their part, they are Christ's obedient and only true church, waiting eagerly for His return.

Thus, while other fundamentalists collaborate in putting pressure on ecclesiastical or political authorities in their fight against modernity, the tight Brethren remain apart from the struggle. In social systems terminology, they are so extremely differentiated that any form of counter-balancing integration is impossible. They are entirely on their own, left to their own resources to quietly and faithfully reproduce their ritual practices without which any religious system dies. Given the ineffectiveness of their evangelism, and the low retention rate of their children within the sect, their future appears uncertain.

SOCIAL AND PSYCHOLOGICAL IMPLICATIONS

It is one of the advantages of liberal multicultural societies that they provide the freedom and opportunity for sectarian groups such as the tight Brethren to practise their piety in their own quiet way. It might be argued that they are a classic example of 'free riders', those who gain the benefits of society without incurring its costs. Given their submission to 'the powers that be', however, and their fulfilment of their statutory obligations, this is a difficult criticism to justify.

Nevertheless, they do not participate in the usual activities of a liberal democracy, such as voting or engaging in dialogue with others. Nor do they add to social capital by joining clubs or supporting voluntary organizations They do not 'Bowl Alone', to quote the memorable title of Robert Putnam's book about declining American community[10]; they do not even bowl at all!

Yet Brethren assemblies do, without doubt, constitute a social and psychological home for many, particularly those who lack family and friends. Brothers and Sisters give and receive acceptance and respect, and are not forgotten when they are old and when they die (see Chap. 6). Moreover, they gain confidence and assurance about their future in this life and the next.

Unfortunately, however, this strong group identity is associated with negative attitudes towards all other social groups to a greater or lesser degree. It also results in a simply structured self-concept, dominated by the assembly identity and ill-suited to life in a complex modern society. While this simple self may not be too great a handicap for the elderly, it is a developmental millstone for the young. Yet adaptation to modern life is certainly not an aim of Brethren parenting (as is consistent with their world view). As I showed in Chap. 7, every effort is made to ensure that the assembly identity is inculcated from the very beginning into Brethren children. Their low retention rates indicate that, unlike the Amish, such efforts are not very successful.

What we can be confident of, however, is that, unlike some other fundamentalist sects, the Brethren are unlikely to embrace authoritarian nationalist populist ideologies: their sole authority is the Bible, their kingdom is not of this world, and their people are the saints waiting to be raptured. No, we are at no risk from the Brethren. It could indeed be argued that they have, on the contrary, performed a service by propounding a comprehensive and uncompromising Protestant fundamentalist world view, and by acting in accordance with it. In so doing, they have forced us to be more aware of the assumptions, values, and practices of modernity.[11] In particular, they have challenged us to confront modernity's failures to fulfil its own prospectus from a religious perspective. Unlike them, however, most will also wish to acknowledge two things: first, modernity's continuing power and immense benefits to humankind[12]; and second, our own identity as modern people.

Summary

Modernity is currently in crisis. It is widely perceived to have ceased delivering on its prospectus. Increasing inequalities have obscured the fact that in global terms, humankind has continued to enjoy better standards of health and well-being than previous generations. Dissatisfaction with apparent lack of progress has resulted in the rise of nationalist populist governments and a distrust of established institutions. The process of differentiation, the essence of modernity, has continued to empower functional social systems, however, and postmodernity is certainly not yet upon us. On the contrary, such systems as business, government, science, and religion each continue to exercise power and influence, both in their own right and in association. But how do the Brethren fit into this account? They are so far differentiated from other social systems that they have little impact, despite their currently fashionable authoritarian culture. However, they do serve to point up modernity's optimistic prospectus by adamantly proclaiming its opposite.

Notes

1. Kumar, Krishan (1995) From Post-Industrial to Post-Modern Society. Oxford: Blackwell.
2. Monbiot, George (2017) Out of the Wreckage: A New Politics for an Age of Crisis. London: Verso.
3. Piketty, Thomas (2014) Capital in the Twenty-First Century. Boston: Harvard University Press.
4. Wilkinson, Richard, & Pickett, Kate (2009) The Spirit Level: Why More Equal Societies Almost Always Do Better. London: Allen Lane.
5. Tegmark, Max (2017) Life 3.0: Being Human in the Age of Artificial Intelligence. London: Allen Lane.
6. Mounk, Yascha (2018) The People vs Democracy: Why Our Freedom is in Danger and How to Save It. Boston: Harvard University Press.
7. Beyer, Peter (2006) Religions in Global Society. London: Routledge.
8. Brown, Ruth (2002) For a Christian America: A History of the Religious Right. New York: Prometheus Books.
9. Warner, Rob (2007) Reinventing English Evangelicalism, 1966–2001. Milton Keynes: Paternoster.
10. Putnam, Robert (2000) Bowling Alone: The Collapse and Revival of American Community. New York: Simon & Schuster.
11. Seligman, Adam (2000) Modernity's Wager: Authority, the Self, and Transcendence. Princeton: Princeton University Press.
12. Pinker, Steven (2018) Enlightenment Now: The Case for Reason, Science, Humanism, and Progress. London: Allen Lane.

CHAPTER 18

Fundamentalism and Christianity

DIFFERENTIATION OF SOCIAL SYSTEMS

The previous argument leads to one inescapable conclusion. We cannot construe fundamentalism as merely an internal theological squabble between religious people. Once we recognize that fundamentalism's real enemy is modernity, then the logic of fundamentalism's hostility to mainstream religion becomes clear. For mainstream religion is itself a product of the modernization process. Like the other functional social systems, religion too has had to differentiate itself and negotiate with them the boundaries of their respective territories. Religion has thus abandoned absolutist claims and, from the fundamentalist perspective, compromised the truth.

Thus, fundamentalists are particularly hostile to mainstream religion not only because it is worldly, like the other social systems, but also because in their view it has betrayed the Almighty, knowing the truth but denying it. What fundamentalists fail to appreciate, however, is that they too are modern, in the sense that they are a reaction against modernity. Without it, they would not have a reason for existing as an alternative to it.

We, therefore, have to ask some historical questions. How has religion become what it is today: a differentiated system within the modern global social system? How has it arrived at its aims, world view, values, and practices? Where and how does it draw the boundaries between itself and the other systems such as government, science, and media? To what extent has it acted alone within its own system and to what extent has it collaborated

© The Author(s) 2018

P. Herriot, *The Open Brethren: A Christian Sect in the Modern World*,
https://doi.org/10.1007/978-3-030-03219-7_18

157

with other systems? And, finally, what damage upon it has the fundamentalist opposition inflicted? Has fundamentalism been more effective in its opposition to mainstream religion than it has to its primary target: modernity in general? I limit the discussion in this chapter to the case of Christianity, using the justification that modernity took root and made early progress in Europe, a predominantly Christian continent.

One popular narrative of the development of modernity runs as follows: The mediaeval world was dominated by the church, which, faced with the challenge of the Enlightenment and the growth of the industrial economy, soon started treating all the rapidly developing social systems as its enemies. Using its facility for binary distinctions, it branded them as worldly (as opposed to spiritual), or secular (as opposed to sacred). In its subsequent struggle to retain as much as it could of its former power, it has grudgingly but repeatedly yielded ground to secularization. The modern world is now largely secular, and looks as though it will progress further in its relegation of religion to the status of a harmless private personal activity.

But this reading of history fails to recognize that religion has transformed itself in association with all the other newly differentiating systems.[1,2] It too has had to define itself as different from science, government, business, law, arts, media, medicine, and so on. Like them, it has had to negotiate its boundaries with regard to its aim, scope, narrative, and practices. This remains even today a tricky task; witness religious dress, established church status, business ethics, faith healing, and social policy, to name but a few currently contested boundary sites.

The social systems are now all functional. To repeat, they are each concerned to fulfil their fundamental purpose: respectively in their order of mention in the previous paragraph, to approach the transcendent, to increase knowledge, to exercise power, to create wealth, to maintain justice, to express emotions, to enable communication, and to improve health. Each of them construes reality in its own terms, develops its peculiar terminology, and constructs its own world view. Moreover, each perceives its activities as self-contained, self-referential, and self-recreating. The task of science is to create knowledge in order to create more knowledge ('more research is needed on this topic'); that of business, to create wealth in order to invest it to create more wealth; that of the law, to make judicial decisions so as to provide a basis for subsequent judicial decisions. And so on.

Each system, then, stands or falls by its own self-defined success. It continuously differentiates itself still further in order to more effectively address and solve the problems and tasks it has created for itself. New academic disciplines are created, administrative regulations proliferate, novel financial instruments are devised, and so on. In sum, social systems feed on themselves.

Thus far, this account gives the false impression that the systems act independently of each other, blithely using their own means in pursuit their own ends. On first acquaintance with an unfamiliar system, this is an entirely understandable reaction. "What on earth are these people talking about?" we sometimes ask ourselves. However, historically, social systems have, on the contrary, continuously interacted with each other. From relatively early in the modern era, for example, nation states and specific Christian denominations supported each other, with Switzerland and Scotland associated with Calvinism, Scandinavia and part of Germany with Lutheranism. Nation states and business corporations have historically had close ties, while both state and corporate entities have supported science and benefitted from the technology which results.

But it is not merely in terms of pooling their resources that social systems have supported each other. They have actually ensured each other's continued existence by recognizing the other and referring to it. The media, for example, have always been full of description and analysis of government, business, and the arts, to the extent that the public's perception of much of the activity and world view of these systems is more mediated than direct. Religion's development has also been facilitated by its recognition in the legislation of nation states. In sum, by acknowledging each other's existence, social systems have ensured their continuance.

Of course, each functional system exercises its authority over its practices and processes largely by means of institutions and organizations. Functional social systems of networked communication are not particularly effective in themselves for purposes of social action and social control. They use institutions and organizations to coordinate and integrate their activities, and also to manage their relationships with other systems.

However, well-established organizations and institutions are only half of the story. To ensure adaptation as well as maintenance, functional systems have sponsored change and innovation through the *social movements* which they permit and often incorporate. With their flexible structure and single purpose, movements can address urgent requirements on the part of institutions to adapt or face the threat of withering away.

CHRISTIANITY AS A FUNCTIONAL SUBSYSTEM

So, how does the social system of religion fit into this historical analysis? Inevitably, religion—in this case Christianity—has come to define itself in terms of its difference from the other systems. Its differentiating feature is its aim to recognize and value the transcendent, and to spread this recognition across the global social system.[3,4] It is therefore unique, in the sense that none of the other systems make such a universal claim, although some might argue that business has succeeded in spreading the values of the market right across the entire global social system (including religion—witness tele-evangelism).

Modern religion does not aim to take over other systems; it is only certain fundamentalisms which work for theocracy or claim superior scientific knowledge. Rather, it asserts the right to have a view on them, to take its own perspective. For example, it might suggest the need for greater humility in science; justice in government; and social responsibility in business.[5] It certainly would not claim to be the only system demonstrating such concerns. But it would be the only one basing them upon an appreciation of the transcendent and its implications for how systems might operate.

This is, unsurprisingly, not a popular stance among other systems, which, like religion itself, guard their boundaries jealously. What right, they often ask, does religion have to interfere? How can it be so arrogant? The fact is that historically they have benefitted from their relationships with religion throughout the modernization process. Religious institutions have provided legitimacy for nation states, which, in return, have provided sanctuary. Religion adapted to such scientific advances as the theory of evolution by developing a theology which incorporated and sanctified it. Religion sponsored social and medical care, education, and artistic expression, helping to save and enrich the lives of citizens in the process. It helped to contain revolutionary movements which sometimes threatened the state (as did Methodism in the UK). Unfortunately, it also periodically opposed those which liberated it (e.g. Catholicism in revolutionary France and, more recently, Spain). Most important, Christianity has recently supported modernity on several human rights issues, for example, slavery and prison reform, despite dragging its feet on issues of women's and gay rights. Governments, for their part, have legislated to guarantee religious freedom, within limits.

But there are other difficulties which modern religion faces, apart from those involved in relating to other systems. To begin with, it is quite hard to discover whether or not religion is achieving its aim. Certainly, it continues to engage in ritual activities which enable adherents to appreciate the transcendent. However, it is not too successful in maintaining this core activity right across individual societies: its degree of success differs immensely between societies and indeed continents (contrast America and Europe).[6]

Moreover, Christianity's institutions have major problems in exercising authority, since, particularly in Protestant Christianity, new sects and movements differentiate out continuously. Hence boundaries are hard to draw. What is authorized religious practice? When does a religious subsystem become an unacceptable cult? How far can individuals' personal religious experiences and choices be permitted to influence organized religious practice?[7] How far can the modern 'inward turn' and desire for personal authenticity drive Christianity's direction?[8] And how can decisions about such issues by the major Christian institutions be enforced?

Religious institutions, moreover, may be struggling to adapt to the speed of societal change. Religious movements urging change can push their own particular vision, sometimes to the benefit and renewal of the system and its institutions, but sometimes to their detriment. Movement leaders frequently ridicule 'stuffy' institutions for maintaining the core activities of worship and service. Charismatic vicars regularly engage in knock-about comedy at the expense of the Church of England, for example.[9] This is a particularly difficult criticism to take for religious institutions, for they do indeed claim to be continuing a tradition (although, in fact, they have often transformed themselves in their effort to survive and adapt).

CHRISTIANITY AND FUNDAMENTALISM

So, in sum, mainstream religion does not have the hard resources of some of the other systems. Nor does it always have their wholehearted support in the struggle against fundamentalism, despite the fact that fundamentalism is a threat to modernity as a whole, not just to mainstream religion. Religion is therefore not in a position to ignore the threat of fundamentalism, which has indeed already caused it considerable damage. This damage is primarily evident in terms of Christianity's relationships with other social systems.

In modernist terminology, the most important damage caused by fundamentalism lies in the *reputational costs* which Christianity has incurred as a result. Fundamentalists have been assiduous in representing themselves as the true, historic, orthodox, and mainstream form of the faith. Indeed, one fundamentalist pressure group in the Church of England has called itself 'Anglican Mainstream'. The media need stories of conflict, and fundamentalists succeed in providing them through their politically astute use of the organizational processes of the institutional church.[10] By carefully choosing their battles, they have succeeded in slowing down institutions' adoption of modern majority positions on minority rights.[11] Consequently, a large proportion of the young now believe the church to be irretrievably and institutionally misogynistic and homophobic.

These perceptions are strengthened by the institutions' difficulties in exercising authority. Once again, the fundamentalists are astute in their choice of issue. In defence of their own and their flocks' tender sensibilities, they refuse to 'have fellowship with' those clergy who break what they say are biblical rules. This 'issue of conscience' permits them to establish organizations through which fundamentalist bishops ordain priests who administer communion to congregations which have been established without consultation. To add insult to injury, they sponsor these activities through an organization named 'Anglican Mission in England'!.[12]

If the church were to exercise its formal disciplinary procedures, however, this would only serve to confirm the fundamentalist narrative of conflict, schism, and persecution. Instead, its strategy has recently been to ensure that discriminatory policies are rejected, and that examples of non-discriminatory practice are publicized. In addition, more positive steps are being taken to support positions which are in accord with modern values, for example, care of the environment, mental health provision, and community solidarity.[13]

More generally, fundamentalists damage Christianity's reputation by their aggressive dealings with the other functional systems. Because they are hostile to the world views, assumptions, and values of all of the other systems, they offend them all. They are despised for their uninformed criticisms of, for example, science and education, and by their absolutist statements of their own position. Given the frequent unfamiliarity with Christianity displayed by scientists and educators, it is easy for the latter to draw general inferences about the faith from the many examples of fundamentalist dogmatism. It is arguable that the influential scientific 'fundamentalism' of the 'new atheists' such as Richard Dawkins is partly the result of their mistaking religious fundamentalism for modern religion.

Fundamentalism, then, is likely to impede the development of dialogue and collaboration between religion and the other functional social systems. As I will argue in the final chapter, such collaboration is crucial for the future of the global social system. But there is another much more mundane impact of fundamentalism on Christianity: *opportunity cost*. It is easy to underestimate the time required to deal with fundamentalists, who are concerned with little else than to instigate and conduct their battles in their war with 'the world'.

All such conflict is the fundamentalists' product. Just as the purpose of research is to generate more research, and that of wealth to create more wealth, so the purpose of fundamentalist conflict is to generate more conflict. By engaging in warfare against them, Christianity is not only helping them to reproduce their raison d'être. It is also missing out on opportunities to show itself open and willing to engage in dialogue and collaboration with other global systems, thereby ensuring its own future.

But the most challenging threat from fundamentalism to modern religion is the *psychological certainty* which it provides to its adherents. It gives them a world view in which a supreme authority both determines what happens in the world and ensures their privileged place both in this world and the world to come. They consequently possess a single dominant social identity which allows them to maintain a high level of self-esteem and a sense of superiority over those not included. It also meets their needs for affiliation and belonging. Most of these outcomes are also offered by authoritarian populist nationalists. But, as I will argue in the final chapter, modern religion, in contrast, cannot possibly offer simple self-concepts based on single social identities, for these do not properly represent the reality of global society.

Summary
Religion is one of the major modern functional social systems. A superficial historical glance reveals immediately that it cannot be dismissed as an increasingly private and minority activity, continuously losing out to the ongoing march of secularism. Such a theoretical approach is based on a Western perspective, biased by a preoccupation with its own situation of decreasing religious adherence and practice. Nevertheless, religion is apparently less successful than the other major global function systems in achieving its own main aim, which is enabling a global appreciation of the transcendent. This is perhaps due to the difficulties of demonstrating success in this somewhat abstract enterprise, and also to problems in defining

its boundaries with other social systems. Fundamentalism, too, constitutes one of modern religion's major impediments. By its opposition to modernity, fundamentalism directly confronts modern social systems, denying their right to exist. Hence the association of fundamentalism with religion results in huge costs to religion in terms of its reputation in the eyes of other systems. It also uses up a lot of its resources in combating it.

NOTES

1. Luhmann, Niklas (1984) Religious Dogmatics and the Evolution of Societies. New York: E. Mellen Press.
2. Beyer, Peter (2006) Religions in Global Society. London: Routledge.
3. Durkheim, Emile (1965) The Elementary Forms of the Religious Life. New York: Free Press.
4. Taves, Ann (2009) Religious Experience Reconsidered. Princeton: Princeton University Press.
5. www.theosthinktank.co.uk
6. Davie, Grace (2002) Europe: The Exceptional Case: Parameters of Faith in the Modern World. London: Darton, Longman, & Todd.
7. Bellah, Robert, Madsen, Richard, Sullivan, William, Swidler, A., & Tipton, Steven. Habits of the Heart (2nd edn). Berkeley CA: University of California Press.
8. Taylor, Charles (2007) A Secular Age. Cambridge MA: Harvard University Press.
9. Herriot, Peter (2016) Warfare and Waves: Calvinists and Charismatics in the Church of England. Eugene OR: Wipf & Stock.
10. Porter, Muriel (2011) Sydney Anglicans and the Threat to World Anglicanism: The Sydney Experiment. Farnham: Ashgate.
11. www.natcen.ac.uk/our-research/research/british-social-attitudes
12. www.anglicanmissioninengland.org
13. Welby, Justin (2018) Reimagining Britain: Foundations for Hope. London: Bloomsbury Press.

CHAPTER 19

Religion and Globalization

Too Different?

From a social systems perspective, we might argue that the present crisis of modernity is due to an imbalance between differentiation and integration. Differentiation has dominated at the cost of integration. Each of the major functional systems has concentrated on its own main aim and purpose, without much reference to the rest of the global social system. The consequence has been that fundamental questions about how their main aim is being achieved, what are the outcomes, and whose interests they serve, or indeed, why such an aim is worth achieving at all, have not been properly addressed.

Consider government, and its currently most visible institution, *the nation state.*[1,2] The aim of gaining power and then exercising it has dominated the activity both of various parties within nation states and of states themselves as international actors. However, their efforts are currently faltering. Most social exchange—for example, of information, or capital, or labour—now occurs on the global rather than the national stage. States' historic control of these flows is now largely lost. The main exercise of power left to them is internally over their citizens and externally in conflict with other powerful nations.

The past decade has seen certain governments persecute, murder, and expel their own citizens. It has also provided many examples of rogue states testing the resolve of other states by breaking the formal rules or the informal norms of international relations. Yet most people still believe that

© The Author(s) 2018

P. Herriot, *The Open Brethren: A Christian Sect in the Modern World,*
https://doi.org/10.1007/978-3-030-03219-7_19

nation states are the only possible basic institution of government. It is hardly surprising, then, that they have turned to 'strong men' and their promises of restored homeland and traditional nationhood as their last chance.[3,4]

Yet these authoritarian totems have little hope of reclaiming political power for the nation state. For technology corporations such as Facebook, Amazon, and Google are gaining control over processes previously the province of government—surveillance, social (dis)order, and political activity. Populist leaders are forced to fight bogus enemies abroad and persecute scapegoats at home in order to bolster the national identity of their citizens.

Which brings us to *business*, another functional system which has pursued its aim—the creation of wealth—with greater success. Yet for all the overall average benefit to billions globally, its disregard for regulation and its absence of ethical compass prompted the reckless risk-taking which threatened to destroy the entire global financial system in 2008.[5] Business in the Anglo-American model typically treats the shareholders as the main, if not the only, stakeholders in the enterprise. In so doing, it is ensuring that the essence of its activity, creating wealth over the short term in order to create more wealth, is secure. Other possible stakeholders such as employees, customers, national economies, or sufferers from climate change come a distant second or are ignored entirely in the quest for short-term returns.[6]

Or take *science and technology*, where the ability to predict and control on the basis of ever increasing knowledge has had amazing success, saving and enriching lives.[7] Yet the immense drive to solve conceptual and technical problems generated from existing knowledge has had some unpredicted consequences. Social media technology has been used to influence the political process without the knowledge of voters, for example.[8] Antibiotics have built up the resistance of the very bacterial infections they were developed to cure. Chemical and biological research has resulted in ever more dangerous weapons of mass destruction.

It is not just failure to predict unexpected outcomes, however, which mars the high reputation of the scientific functional system. It is also the relative lack of attention to the grounds for choosing research topics and agendas. What should we be researching, and why? And what of the even more fundamental issues looming on the horizon? What, for example, does the development of artificial intelligence to a level equal or superior to that of human beings imply for the very notion of being human?[9]

The same critique can be applied to other functional social systems, which all seem to concentrate on their own aim of reproducing themselves without much reference to other perspectives; "art for art's sake", for example, or the upholding of the law at the expense of social justice. Yet differentiated systems do nevertheless relate to other systems. Business and government are frequent partners, as are business and science, and government and law. Historically, and still occasionally today, religion and government are in alliance.

However, it could be argued that the primary purpose of all of these partnerships is to enable each party to better achieve its own aim. Business needs an ordered social environment within which to create wealth, and government needs the taxes which business and customers pay. Science needs funding to conduct research and develop technologies, while government and business need these technologies to fulfil their social contract with their citizens or to make a profit. Historically, and sometimes still today, religion needed protection, while government needed the legitimacy which religion provided.

It is much more difficult, however, to think of partnership situations in which systems collaborate to address issues which do not directly further their primary aims. Such issues are often those which face the global social system as a whole: climate change, for example, or obscene inequalities of wealth, or pockets of abject poverty, or war and persecution.

Another obstacle to integration is the disproportionate and unaccountable power of the institutions and organizations of certain functional systems relative to the others. In particular, global business and technology, and above all, these two in conjunction, technological business, have gained sudden and startling power. Stalin may or may not have threatened to park his tanks on the Pope's lawn, but today, governments and civil society are justly fearful of Facebook's algorithms.

RELIGION AND GLOBALIZATION

The essence of *globalization* is that it is a continuing process resulting in a global social system. This process may be understood in terms of a communicative network, which develops as a result of a continuous interchange between global and local networks.[10] Local communications may reach and shape global discourse, and the reverse also occurs. An article in a specialized scientific journal can cast doubt on a globally accepted theoretical paradigm; a single communal ecstatic religious experience can inspire a global charismatic movement. And conversely, a global trend towards nationalistic rhetoric can lead to immigrant families discussing their future with anxiety; and world trends in energy prices can result in the demise of small local businesses.

Excessive differentiation implies communicative silos, where neither at local nor at global levels do the functional social systems communicate with each other. Yet widely shared concern for the common good, perception of a common fate, and awareness of a common humanity,[11] are pushing them to do so. So in the midst of the current crisis in modernity, how might such increased integration be promoted? And, specifically, what role has religion to play in the process?

Like the other systems, modern religion has differentiated out into a myriad of subsystems. It has concentrated on its main aim: relating to the transcendent through its institutions and practices. It has sought to ensure its own survival and growth by means of evangelism and new organizations and movements. While faltering in Europe, it enjoys considerable global success in these terms.[12]

Religion's relations with other systems, however, have been fraught with problems for a variety of reasons. It has often disputed boundary areas (for example, in medicine) or directly challenged expertise (in natural and social science). It has sometimes arrogantly assumed that its own truth and the criteria it uses to determine it should apply equally in the other systems. It has defended its reputation rather than its victims in varied abuse scandals. And it has tended to lump all the other systems together into an undifferentiated 'Other', labelled 'secularism'. It is certainly not the activities of fundamentalists alone which have caused this reputational damage.

However, over and against this criticism, modern religion has consistently allied with voluntary advocacy organizations to address issues of injustice and inequality. It has carefully identified the key issues and cases in which to intervene, realizing that its actions are closely observed and are interpreted as indicating its values and beliefs. Examples are its attacks on pay-day lenders; its support for disabled people losing benefit payments; and its protests at the inhuman treatment of some immigrants. It has also specified its theological grounds for such action—for example, in the Declarations following from Vatican 2, especially *Dignitatis Humanae* (Of Human Dignity) and *Gaudium et Spes* (Joy and Hope).

But these activities are merely nibbling at the edge of the immense possibilities for religion arising from globalization. Religion has three precious assets which could potentially contribute to global society. First, because of its appreciation of the transcendent, it expressly places a high value on humility and compassion. Second, it reaches and represents a constituency, the poorer and less fortunate parts of humanity, which often feel themselves alienated from the other systems. And finally, it shares with moral philosophy the simple golden rule to 'do as you would be done by', which respects everyone equally as a fellow human being.

Religion may not be widely perceived in these terms at present. But it can urgently speak by its actions and its words to change perceptions. It could approach the institutions, organizations and movements of other social systems in an attitude of humility, seeking to discover what are the key issues *they* believe to be facing humanity and to understand why they place such a priority upon them. The science, arts, and legal systems, in particular, appear to be fruitful potential partners for extended dialogue. Religion could also claim an ability to enlist support from parts other systems find it hard to reach. And it could demonstrate a degree of moral authority to facilitate these contacts and the increased collaboration which could follow. Neither at the local nor the global level should such soft power be underestimated, magnified as it is by global networks and by the fading authority of the nation state.

The global-local dialectic of globalization reminds us also of the most local actor of all: the individual. All sociological analysis in terms of social systems needs to be supported by psychological analysis at the individual level if social change is to be adequately understood. Any inter-systemic relations have to be represented in the social identity system of the self if global communication is actually to occur. Single dominant social identities characterize the self-concepts of people who operate only in terms of a single differentiated social subsystem: fundamentalist believers, for example, or single-minded scientists. Multiple and complex social identities, however, are typically to be found in the self-concepts of the many modern people who engage both within and between different social systems.

Their personal struggle is, of course, how to construct a self-concept which integrates their varied social identities, just as the issue for global society is how better to integrate differentiated social systems. Just as social systems have to engage in meaningful dialogue, so individuals have to engage in an internal dialogue if they are to relate their several social identities with each other: social scientist, citizen, and Christian, for example. To discover a sense of personal wholeness and integrity in an excessively differentiated world is indeed a hard task. It is, however, a problem towards the solution of which religion has a major contribution to make.

MY FATHER'S BIBLE AGAIN

It is a far cry indeed from the Brethren to an integrated world and an integrated, but complex, self. Hopefully, however, I have shown that they are not totally unrelated, but are rather the precise obverse of each other. The Brethren are at the extreme edge of the religious system, reacting vigorously against the slightest hint of integration with any other social system, even with the fundamentalist evangelical wing of Christianity from which they separated. From the psychological perspective, the Brethren self is just that—dominated by the single Brethren social identity which regulated action in every social situation.

Modern religion, on the other hand (Christianity in this case) is eagerly beginning to operate in global society. This means it has to connect upwards and across within its own system, and outwards to other systems at local and global levels. Instead of the Brethren's isolationist and absolutist yearning for authority and purity, modern Christianity can demonstrate a degree of humility and vulnerability in the face of the transcendent which the other social systems do not often emulate. Hence religious people have to develop complex and multifaceted selves to act within global society, yet they must also advocate that there are some boundaries to human endeavour which it would be wise to observe. This difficult balancing act we will only achieve if we develop a more profound view of what it means to be a human being.[13]

Summary

Modernity's current crisis could be attributed to the continued differentiation of functional systems in their effort to achieve their own aims. Success in such achievement is of undoubted benefit to humankind. However, pursuit of particular aims with little regard to the aims of other systems has multiple unpredicted and often harmful consequences. Differentiation has to be balanced by integration if the world's current pressing problems are to be addressed successfully. Modern religion could facilitate such integration at the local and global levels. Religion possesses several important elements of soft power. Its visionary appreciation of the transcendent engenders a degree of humility which could temper overweening ambition and facilitate open-minded dialogue; its identification with the poor gives it an advocacy role on behalf of a neglected constituency; and its respect for the universal human condition is expressed in the appealing golden rule of 'do as you would be done by'. But any religious input to dialogue at the local and global levels depends ultimately upon individuals with complex selves. Dialogue between social systems requires internal dialogue in minds which embrace multiple social identities. Fundamentalist identities are distinctly unhelpful.

NOTES

1. Ohmae, Kenichi (1995) The End of the Nation State: The Rise of Regional Economies. New York: Simon & Schuster.
2. Holton, Robert (2011) Globalization and the Nation State (2nd edn) Basingstoke: Palgrave Macmillan.
3. Moffitt, Benjamin (2016) The Global Rise of Populism: Performance, Political Style, and Representation. Stanford CA: Stanford University Press.
4. Albertazzi, Daniele, & McDonnell, Duncan (2008) Twenty-First Century Populism: The Spectre of Western European Democracy. Basingstoke: Palgrave Macmillan.
5. Herriot, Peter (2016) All in this Together? Identity, Politics, and Church in Austerity Britain. London: Darton, Longman, & Todd.
6. Pilketty, Thomas (2014) Capital in the Twenty-First Century. Cambridge MA: Belknap Press.
7. Pinker, Stephen (2018) Enlightenment Now: London: Allen Lane.
8. *The Guardian*, March 25th 2018.
9. Harari, Yuval (2015) Homo Deus: A Brief History of Tomorrow. London: Vintage.
10. Robertson, Roland (1992) Globalization: Social Theory and Global Culture. London: Sage.
11. Scholte, Jan (2005) Globalization: A Critical Introduction (2nd edn) Basingstoke: Palgrave Macmillan.
12. Davie, Grace (2002) Europe: The Exceptional Case. London: Darton, Longman, & Todd.
13. www.togetherforthecommongood.co.uk

GLOSSARY

Adversary, the Satan
Assemblies, the The Open Brethren
Assembly, an A local Brethren congregation
Assembly truth Beliefs about correct assembly practice
Believers Brethren
Believers' baptism Baptism by immersion
Bema God's throne on judgement day
Born-again Saved, converted to evangelical Christianity
Breaking of Bread Holy Communion
Brethren Evangelical Protestant movement from the 1820s
Brethren Male Brethren
Brothers Male Brethren
Burdening Worrying
Called home Died
Cast upon the Lord Unsure what to do
Chastening Punishment
Christendom 'False' 'Christian' beliefs & organisations
'Christian' Christian
Church age The current dispensation (period of history)
Coming out Leaving the 'sects' and joining the Brethren
Communicating brother Invites visiting preachers
Consistent Regularly attends at assembly meetings
Conviction of sin Feeling guilty

© The Author(s) 2018

173

P. Herriot, *The Open Brethren: A Christian Sect in the Modern World*,
https://doi.org/10.1007/978-3-030-03219-7

Dispensations Historical periods of God's relationship with humankind
End times The future as revealed in biblical prophecy
Esteemed Highly reputed in the Brethren
Exercised Concerned about
Exclusive Brethren Sect formed after Brethren schism of 1848
Faithful Regularly attends at assembly meetings
False What we disagree with
False brethren Brethren who believe differently from us
False religions Non-Christian religions
False profession Saying you are saved when you are not
False shepherds Leaders who believe differently from us
Fellowship, in Being a member of a Brethren assembly
Full-time out in the work Full-time preacher
Gathering to the name of the Lord alone Brethren
Giving a word Preaching
Glory, in Dead
God's Word The Bible
Going out in faith Full-time preacher without a regular income
Gospel, the Salvation by faith in Christ's atonement for our sin
Gospel hall Brethren chapel
Gospel meeting Service aimed at converting the unsaved
Headship The superordinate role of brothers over sisters
Helpmeet Wife
Home, at home with the Lord Dead
Home-call Death
Inerrancy Without error (of the Bible)
Inspiration, verbal Belief God inspired every word of the Bible
Last times The future as revealed in biblical prophecy
Led of the Lord Decided to
Letter of commendation Vouching for a Brother's soundness
Loose Brethren Liberal faction of the Open Brethren
Lord's day Sunday
Lord's Supper Holy Communion
Meeting, a A Brethren service
Meeting, the The assembly
Meetings, the The Open Brethren
Millennium, the Christ's thousand-year rule on earth
Ministry meeting Service of Bible teaching for the assembly
Modesty Appropriate dress and demeanour for sisters

Morality Sexual relationships
Old Man, the The human condition prior to salvation
Open Brethren Sect formed after Brethren schism of 1848
Original sin Inherited by everyone from Adam
Overseers (See 'oversight')
Oversight, the The Brothers leading an assembly
Portion, daily A passage from the Bible for the day
Premillennial Belief the rapture will occur before millennium
Putting out the fleece Waiting for a sign from God
Quiet time Daily period of personal prayer and Bible study
Rapture Christ's bodily return to take the saved up to heaven
Reception Acceptance into assembly fellowship
Remnant Faithful followers of Christ throughout history
Rituals Human perversions of Scriptural worship
Saints Brethren
Saved Converted to evangelical Christianity
Scriptures, the The Bible
Scriptures Verses from the Bible
Sects, the Christian denominations
Secular employment Not full-time out in the work
Sinner Not saved
Sister Female Brother
Sound (adj) Holds the same beliefs as us
Subject (adj) Proper relation of the Sister to the Brother
Submission Proper relation of the Sister to the Brother
Swanwick Conferences held by the loose Brethren
Taking part Contributing to worship at the Lord's Supper
Testimony, the The local assembly
Testimony, giving Recounting one's Brethren history
Tight Brethren The conservative faction of the Open Brethren
Tribulation, the Seven years of suffering after the rapture
Unbelievers Those not saved
Unequally yoked together Doing things with non-Brethren
Whole counsel of God, the Assembly truth
With the Lord Dead
Witnessing Preaching to the unsaved by word or deed
World, the All social systems other than the Brethren

SUBJECT INDEX

© The Author(s) 2018   177
P. Herriot, *The Open Brethren: A Christian Sect in the Modern World*,
https://doi.org/10.1007/978-3-030-03219-7

BIBLICAL INDEX

G
Genesis
  2.17, 93
  19.4-7, 98

L
Leviticus
  18.22, 98

J
Judges
  6, 68

E
Esther 1.1, 55

P
Psalms
  16.11, 57
  40.3, 52
Proverbs 13.24, 87

J
Jeremiah
  17.9, 114

D
Daniel, 78

Z
Zephaniah
  3.17, 3

M
Matthew
  16.15, 14

L
Luke
  4-10, 5

© The Author(s) 2018

193

P. Herriot, *The Open Brethren: A Christian Sect in the Modern World*,
https://doi.org/10.1007/978-3-030-03219-7

Printed by Printforce, the Netherlands